Surviving the Blockade of Leningrad

Svetlana Magayeva
Albert Pleysier

Translated into English and edited by
Alexey Vinogradov

UNIVERSITY PRESS OF AMERICA,® INC.
Lanham • Boulder • New York • Toronto • Oxford

Copyright © 2006 by
University Press of America,® Inc.
4501 Forbes Boulevard
Suite 200
Lanham, Maryland 20706
UPA Acquisitions Department (301) 459-3366

PO Box 317
Oxford
OX2 9RU, UK

Library of Congress Control Number: 2006925039
ISBN-13: 978-0-7618-3420-5 (clothbound : alk. paper)
ISBN-10: 0-7618-3420-6 (clothbound : alk. paper)
ISBN-13: 978-0-7618-3421-2 (paperback : alk. paper)
ISBN-10: 0-7618-3421-4 (paperback : alk. paper)

∞™ The paper used in this publication meets the minimum
requirements of American National Standard for Information
Sciences—Permanence of Paper for Printed Library Materials,
ANSI Z39.48—1992

The book is dedicated to all the people who died
in Leningrad during the siege.

Contents

Maps

Svetlana as a young girl.

Authors' Preface

In June 1941 the Soviet Union found itself at war against Germany and Finland. Within less than three months the German military forces who invaded the Soviet Union from the west and the Finnish troops who attacked from the north had succeeded in establishing a blockade around Leningrad. The siege of this Soviet city would last almost nine hundred days and during that time Leningrad was struck by incessant aerial bombing and artillery fire from long-range guns. The winter of 1941–1942 was particularly severe for the city's inhabitants. A shortage of fuel in the city forced the people to attempt to keep warm by wearing their overcoats and huddling around their small wood burning stoves. The winter was the coldest in more than a century. The freezing temperatures caused the pipes of the city's water system to burst and thereafter the people acquired their water from the rivers that flowed through the city and from neighborhood canals. What was most devastating was the shortage of food. In November the daily ration of bread was 250 grams for workers in the factories and 125 grams for dependents and children. People ate whatever they believed would give them nourishment; that included pets, rats and even the cadavers of human beings. The blockade around the city came to an end in early 1944 but by that time more than a million Leningraders had lost their lives.

Svetlana Magayeva and her mother were residents of Leningrad at the time the Soviet Union was invaded. In the early months of the siege the two tried to maintain a lifestyle that was similar to the one experienced previous to the blockade. Svetalana continued her education with a teacher and her mother, herself an educator, fulfilled the duties to which she was assigned by the city officials. The German air raids, the enemy artillery shelling, the freezing temperatures and the starvation due to a shortage of food would so weaken their bodies that they were placed under the care of others. Svetalana was brought to a children's house and her mother was confined to a hospital for adults.

At the children's house Svetlana would be influenced forever by the people who worked there and by the children for whom they cared. Most of the children had been orphaned by the war. A large percentage of these children would not survive the siege in spite of the care they received from the nurses and doctors who had been assigned to the house. Some children would suffer from the abuse of other children and some would benefit from the support of those who became their friends. Each child was unique, yet they all shared the shelling, the air raids, the pangs of hunger and the death that devastated Leningrad. Svetlana witnessed people committing acts of heroism and human beings demonstrating compassion and love for others under the most difficult circumstances. The book is an effort to honor these human beings and at the same time record their actions so they will not be forgotten.

The authors believed that the events witnessed by Svetlana and her mother needed to be recognized in their historical context. Therefore, the text is preceded with a brief history of the siege. The reader is introduced to the political events that would bring the Soviet Union at war against Germany and Finland. Before the German and Finnish forces were able to establish a blockade around Leningrad, the political and military leadership of the city made decisions that would call into action the city's residents including Svetlana's mother. Discussed are the disastrous effects that the siege would have on Svetlana and her mother and the other citizens. In a desperate move to save Leningrad from starvation, the city officials created a route across Lake Ladoga that would be used to bring food and other supplies into the besieged city. The route would be modified with the changing seasons and the actions of those who were associated with the route are described. It was this lifeline that saved the lives of hundreds of thousands of Leningraders. It was also this lifeline that was used to bring Svetlana and her mother out of the besieged city.

Acknowledgement

We wish to thank Elena Martilla for giving us permission to use one of her drawings as the cover for the book. Elena is a native of Leningrad and was eighteen years old when the Germans and Finns established a blockade around the city in 1941. During the siege of the city, Elena would continue her schooling in art and would record through drawings and paintings the human suffering she witnessed. The drawing on the cover of the book shows a young girl facing a wood stove on which she is heating water in a kettle. In her hands she is holding a treasured plant that she has managed to keep alive. In the background each window of the apartment has been reinforced with two strips of tape that have been applied in a crossing pattern. This was done to prevent the windows from breaking during an enemy bombing raid or artillery shelling.

Introduction:
The Siege of Leningrad

The blockade around Leningrad during World War II was established in 1941 by German forces who invaded the Soviet Union from the west and by Finnish troops that advanced on the city from the north. The siege of the city would last almost nine hundred days. During that time the Germans struck Leningrad with incessant aerial bombing and with artillery fire from long-range guns. The winter of 1941–1942 was particularly severe and the coldest in more than a century. A shortage of fuel in the city reduced the power supply, adversely affecting heating, lighting and cooking. The cold temperatures caused the pipes of the water system to burst and thereafter the rivers that flowed through the city and the canals became the people's sources of water. What was most devastating was the shortage of food. Supplies were airlifted into Leningrad, but they were insufficient to feed the people. In November the daily ration of bread was 250 grams for workers in factories and 125 grams for dependents and children. People ate whatever they could find to stay alive; this included pets, birds, rats, carpenter's glue and castor oil. The freezing temperatures, however, deepened the ice that covered Lake Ladoga located east of the city and made it possible to create an organization of ice roads across the lake. Food and other supplies were brought from the Russian mainland to the east shore of the lake and transported across the ice roads and into Leningrad. The Road of Life, as it was called, saved the city, but thousands of its people would die from starvation during the first winter of the siege. The blockade around the city came to end in early 1944, but by that time more than a million Leningraders had lost their lives.

The attack on Leningrad was the culmination of a series of events that began in 1933. In that year the National Socialist German Workers' Party became the largest political party in the Reichstag, the lower house of

Germany's Parliament, and the party's leader, Adolph Hitler, was appointed Chancellor. Shortly thereafter, the deputies in the Reichstag passed the Enabling Act which gave the new Chancellor dictatorial power. Hitler hated the Marxist socialist ideology and Communists and would use his newly acquired political power to destroy the Communist movement in Germany. He also told the German citizenry that Germany needed "lebensraum" and that this living space would be acquired from the Soviet Union.

Hitler's actions against the German Communists and the fear that the Soviet Union might become a victim of Hitler's designs caused Joseph Stalin to try and protect Communist Russia through collective security. In September 1934, the Soviet Union entered the League of Nations. The Soviet delegate to the League of Nations, Maxim Litvinov, quickly became a defender of universal disarmament and an advocate for punishing nations that carried out acts of aggression. In 1935 the Soviet Union signed pacts with France and Czechoslovakia. These treaties stated that if the League of Nations certified that Czechoslovakia had become a victim of German acts of aggression, the Soviet Union would come to the aid of the Czechs. Soviet aid would be forthcoming only after the French, who were bound to the Czechs by a long standing alliance, honored their obligations first. But the French along with the British failed to support Czechoslovakia when Hitler demanded Czech lands at the Munich Conference held in September of 1938. The two western powers had also failed to stand up to Germany's violations of the Versailles Treaty ever since 1934. Stalin decided that he could not rely on the French and British to stop Hitler's Germany.

Convinced that collective security was no longer an option, Stalin worked at improving relations with Hitler hoping to postpone a German invasion of the Soviet Union. In May 1939, Litvinov, who was Jewish, was replaced by Viacheslav Molotov as People's Commissar for Foreign Affairs. Stalin also ordered Molotov to remove all Jews from his ministry. The changes forecasted a new direction in Soviet foreign policy. In June, a Soviet diplomat in Berlin informed the German government that his country was willing to enter into a nonaggression pact with Germany. Hitler was eager to join the Soviets in such an agreement. He was ready to start a war with Poland and hoped to prevent French and British intervention by depriving them of any assistance from the Soviet Union.

A nonaggression pact was signed between Germany and the Soviet Union on August 23, 1939. The two powers agreed not to attack each other and to remain neutral should either be attacked by a third party. A secret territorial protocol in the pact marked out Lithuania and western Poland as the German sphere of interest. Eastern Poland, Latvia, Estonia, Finland and Bessarabia—still a part of Rumania—were marked as the Soviet sphere of interest. Stalin was pleased with the pact. The secret territorial protocol gave the Soviet Union the opportunity to recover lands that Russia had lost during World War I and its aftermath. At the same time, the pact gave Stalin the time he needed to build up Soviet military and industrial strength for the inevitable attack from Germany.

In September German and Soviet military forces invaded Poland with the understanding that upon Poland's defeat Germany would take control of the western half of that nation, and the Soviet Union would take the eastern half. The war against Poland began on the first day of the month when the Germans invaded from the west. The initial phase of the attack was carried out from the air as the German Luftwaffe destroyed Poland's small air force, and German dive bombers demolished rear guard communications and spread terror among the civilian population. The next phase of the attack was initiated by heavy tanks that were followed by lighter armored divisions. After tearing through the Polish lines, the German motorized columns streaked across Poland's flat lands, often several days ahead of the main body of German infantry. On September 17, two weeks after France and Great Britain had declared war on Germany for its invasion of Poland, Stalin sent Soviet forces into eastern Poland. By the end of the month Polish resistance had collapsed.

Stalin feared that Hitler would next order his forces against the Soviet Union and felt that measures needed to be taken to secure Russia's western borders from a military attack. He quickly forced Estonia, Latvia and Lithuania to agree to mutual assistance pacts under which the Soviet Union was given military, air and naval bases in the Baltic states. (The secret territorial protocol in the Soviet-German nonaggression pact, signed back in August 1939, had marked Lithuania in the German sphere of interest; however, following Poland's defeat Lithuania was made a part of the Soviet sphere of interest). In June 1940, the Soviet leadership accused the Baltic states of violating their mutual assistance pacts with the Soviet Union. They demanded that new governments must be established in the Baltic states, governments that would respect the mutual assistance pacts and permit Soviet troops free access to the Baltic territories. Elections were held in all three countries in July and immediately thereafter the newly elected governments agreed to incorporate their states in the Soviet Union. Estonia, Latvia and Lithuania, which had been created out of Russian provinces at the close of World War I, were now made republics in the Union of Soviet Socialist Republics.

In an attempt to further secure Russia's western borders, Stalin invited neighboring Finland to discuss "concrete political questions." In the negotiations that followed, Stalin requested that Finland cede to the Soviet Union small parcels of territory, including the naval base of Hango on the northern shore of the Gulf of Finland. From the naval base the Soviets would be able to block off the Gulf of Finland from German naval forces and protect Leningrad. In exchange for his requests, Stalin offered to give to Finland about eight thousand eight hundred square kilometers (5,456 square miles) of Karelia along the Finnish border; it was an area of land that was twice the size that Stalin was requesting from Finland. The talks were reported to Finland's population and they, like their government, were opposed to the Soviet Union's proposals. The Finns felt that Stalin's offer was merely a first step in subjugating Finland. The Soviet leadership believed that Finland's rejection of their offer indicated that the Finns planned to assist Hitler's Germany in a future war against the Soviet Union.

On November 30, 1939, the Soviet forces attacked Finland by land, sea and air. The leadership of the Soviet Union claimed that previous to the attack the Finns had shelled the Soviet border killing several Russian soldiers. Thereafter, the Soviet Union had demanded that the Finnish army be withdrawn some twenty-five kilometers (sixteen miles) from their southern border and when the government of Finland refused to comply, the Soviet forces were ordered to attack. Soviet ground forces, about 600,000, were assigned to break through the Mannerheim Line, a strongly fortified zone, some thirty-two kilometers (twenty miles) deep, running diagonally across the Karelian Isthmus. It was the basis of the Finnish defense system and here much of the Finnish artillery and infantry, numbering some 300,000, was concentrated. In December the Soviet assault was stopped on the Mannerheim Line, and by the end of the month the Finns had dealt the Soviets a series of humiliating military defeats. By the beginning of January the Soviet military command had been reorganized, and intensive preparations for a new military offensive were being made. Masses of tanks and heavy field guns and more than a million men were assembled. Throughout the month of January the Soviet air force and artillery bombarded the Mannerheim fortifications. On February 11, the Soviet ground forces were ordered to advance, and five days later they breached the Mannerheim Line. The breach led to a series of Finish retreats, and by early March the Finnish army was on the verge of collapse.

The war came to end officially with the Moscow Peace Treaty which was signed on March 12, 1940. By the terms of the peace agreement, Finland was forced to give the Soviet Union land along its southeastern border including its second largest city, Viipuri (Vyborg). It ceded to the Soviet Union islands in the Gulf of Finland, and the base of Hango was to be leased to the Soviet Union for thirty years. Finland also ceded land in the Salla sector in northeastern Finland and a part of the Rybachiy Peninsula in the Petsamo area. The territories that Finland was forced to relinquish were one-tenth of the country's land mass, and they contained its best agricultural soil. Twelve percent of Finland's population lived there, and only a few hundred would stay. The other more than 400,000 people gave up their homes and property and moved to Finnish held territory. Through war against Finland and with a treaty Stalin had attained his objectives; the Soviet Union acquired naval bases in the Gulf of Finland and Finnish lands that were located close to and north of Leningrad.

In June 1940 Stalin demanded of Romania the province of Bessarabia and northern Bukovina. The province of Bessarabia had been taken from the Soviet Union after World War One. Bukovina was not a Russian territory, but it had a large Ukrainian population and was strategically valuable. Hitler had expected the Soviet Union to seize Bessarabia but not Bukovina for it had not been mentioned in the Soviet-German nonaggression pact. Germany permitted the seizure, but this was as far as Hitler was willing to cooperate with Stalin in eastern Europe. Hitler had found it expedient to sign a nonaggression pact with Stalin, but he never abandoned his plans for an eventual attack on the Soviet Union.

On June 22, 1941, the German forces invaded the Soviet Union and began what Russians would call the Great Patriotic War. The invasion was carried out by German armies designated as Army Group South, directed toward Kiev, Army Group Center, directed toward Moscow, and Army Group North, directed toward Leningrad. The latter was ordered to invade and take control of Kronstadt, the Soviet Baltic republics and their ports and the city of Leningrad in order to deprive the Soviet fleet of its naval bases. Army Group North consisted of a half million men divided into thirty divisions, six of them armored and motorized, and an air fleet of four hundred and thirty airplanes. By July 10, 1941, the Germans had seized almost all of the areas belonging to the Soviet Baltic republics and had entered the region south of Leningrad. Germany's leadership in charge of the military offensive believed that they would experience little difficulty taking Leningrad.

The defense of Leningrad was the responsibility of several men. Marshal Kliment Voroshilov in early July was made the chief of the Leningrad High Command and shortly thereafter Andrie Zhdanov was named his co-commander within the Leningrad Military Council. Zhdanov was the chief of the Leningrad Communist Party organization. At the Smolny complex located along the Neva River in Leningrad, Marshal Voroshilov and Zhdanov planned strategy for the city's defense. To this headquarters top military commanders of the Leningrad Front were summoned and given orders. It was at Smolny that Zhdanov would meet with the city officials upon whom he relied to enforce the defense measures. The chief of these officials was Peter Popkov, Mayor of Leningrad. All day and every day at Smolny the Leningrad Military Council would have conferences with military commanders, Party workers, engineers and specialists. At the end of the day or at night the Smolny headquarters would receive a call from Stalin in Moscow. He would demand a report on the military situation in and around Leningrad. He would also give further directives to those he held responsible for the city's defense.

Zhdanov was directed to create a people's militia that was to join the Soviet military forces who were organizing a defense line south of Leningrad in an attempt to stop the German advance on the city. Originally, it was decided that the militia, better known as the People's Volunteers, should consist of fifteen divisions made up of workers, students and teachers. Party recruiting officers visited the city's factories, shops and offices and called for the workers to do their patriotic duty and join the People's Volunteers. At the Kirov Works alone some 15,000 workers applied for military service. In early July three divisions of volunteers led by military commanders were rushed south to the so-called Luga Line, a line of defense about 282 kilometers (175 miles) long. It ran from Narva located near the Gulf of Finland coast southeast to Kingisepp and then along the Luga River through Luga city to Shimsk at Lake Ilmen (See Map 1—Page 27). By July 7 two more divisions of volunteers had been rushed to the Luga Line and in the days that followed still more divisions were sent south to stop the German military advance. Most of the volunteers had been given only a few days of military training in the main squares of the city, most were inexperienced in military matters and many were inadequately supplied. Despite a shortage of military hardware, the volunteers formed into anti-tank destroyer groups using anti-tank grenades and anti-tank mines. The volunteers and the Soviet forces were able to stop the German military advance at the Luga Line for almost a month, but the majority of the more than 130,000 who joined the People's Volunteers never returned home.

Hundreds of thousands of civilians were recruited to build defense lines and fortifications outside of Leningrad in order to stop the enemy's drive toward the city. Alexie Kuznetsov, deputy to Zhdanov and a member of the Leningrad Military Council, was ordered to direct the construction of the defenses. Able bodied males between the ages of sixteen and fifty years and women between the ages of sixteen and forty-five years were ordered to participate in the construction of the defenses. They were assembled in the city's parks and squares with pick axes, shovels and any other tool that was available, were loaded on a train or on trucks and were brought south to construct two major defense lines between the outskirts of Leningrad and the Luga Line. One ran from the mouth of the Luga River to Chudovo, Gatchina, Uritsk and Pulkovo and then along the Neva River. The second extended from the Peterhof to Gatchina, Pulkovo, Kolpino and Koltushski. Several more defense lines were constructed in the immediate vicinity of the city including one in the northern suburbs facing the Finns. Industrial workers, students, housewives, scientists, teachers, artists and actors worked side by side from morning to night. When one project was completed they would be brought to the next site where they would begin again. Altogether they succeeded in digging more than six hundred kilometers (372 miles) of anti-tank ditches and more than fifteen thousand kilometers (9,300 miles) of open trenches. They erected almost 644 kilometers (400 miles) of barbed wire defenses and 306 kilometers (190 miles) of forest obstacles. Placed within and behind the defenses were gun and machine-gun pillboxes made of reinforced concrete.

The efforts of the People's Volunteers as well as the civilians who constructed the defense lines slowed the German advance and gave the city and Party authorities time to carry out important evacuations. Before the war, Leningrad was one of the most important centers for industrial production in the Soviet Union. In an effort to devote the city's factories toward the national war effort and at the same time take them out of harms way, an evacuation of Leningrad's industries was carried out in July and August. By the end of July the Nevsky machine-building plant had been loaded onto 180 freight cars and sent to Sverdlovsk in the Ural region. The Russian diesel plant had been moved on seventy railway cars to Gorky. The equipment of the Kirov machine plant had been sent on eighty-one cars to Barnaul. By the end of August nearly one hundred industrial plants had been evacuated from the city either in whole or in part. At the same time thousands of skilled industrial workers and their families were sent out of the city by railroad and brought to industrial centers that were being created in the interior. The skilled workers were joined by highly educated professionals who were employees at Leningrad's research institutions.

Evacuation of the city's works of art was also carried out. At the Hermitage, the largest museum in the Soviet Union, staff members and volunteers worked day and night to pack the museum's treasures into crates to be transported to Sverdlovsk. The first train of crates left on June 30 and contained nearly half a million articles. When the articles reached their destination they were stored in three locations: an art gallery, a church and the basement of the Ipiatev Mansion. The latter was the mansion where Tsar Nicholas II and his family were housed before they were executed in 1918. The second train carried 1,422 crates and they contained nearly 700,000 articles. They were evacuated on July 20 and fourteen members of the museum staff accompanied the treasures. The articles for the third train were still being packed when the Germans cut the railroad connections between Leningrad and the rest of the country. These treasures were moved to the cellars of the Hermitage where they would be watched daily by the museum's staff members.

Art treasures and monuments that could not be evacuated were either hidden or camouflaged. Trenches were dug under the linden trees in the Summer Garden, and the eighteenth-century marble statues of Greek goddesses and gods that adorned the garden were buried in them. Sculptor Pyotr Klodt's four bronze horses were taken off their pedestals on Anichkov Bridge and buried in the gardens of the Young Pioneers' palace. Cliff climbers and Alpinists covered the golden spires of the Admiralty building and St. Peter and Paul Cathedral with camouflage cloths. The dome of St. Isaac's Cathedral was coated with gray paint. The statue of Vladimir Lenin in front of the Finland Station and the Bronze Horseman, the equestrian statue of Peter the Great on the embankment of the Neva River, were surrounded with bags filled with sand and then covered with boards and logs. The trees in the city's parks and gardens were declared protected and would remain untouched even during the upcoming winter when there was a shortage of firewood.

Much was done to secure Leningrad and its inhabitants, but mistakes were also made and one of these mistakes placed many children of Leningrad in harms way. Parents were concerned about the safety of their children especially if the enemy should strike the city with air raids. In late June and early July a few trainloads of children were evacuated to Yaroslavl, northeast of Moscow. Many more children were brought by train to vacation spots such as Pskov, Novgorod, Gotchina and Luga located to the south. At the same time the German forces, in their drive toward Leningrad, were approaching the communities to which the children had been brought. Shortly after their arrival, the children had to be hurried away; they were transported back to Leningrad in order to avoid their capture by the enemy. After some time had passed, some of these children along with thousands of others were transported east to places such as Kirovsk and Sverdlovsk.

On August 12, Hitler ordered Army Group North to encircle Leningrad and advance north into the Karelian Isthmus to link up with Finnish troops who were coming down from the north. On the twenty–first of August 1941, the Germans captured Chudovo, thus breaking the railway link between Leningrad and Moscow. On the thirtieth of August they captured the railroad junction at the town of Mga, located nineteen kilometers (12 miles) below the southwest corner of Lake Ladoga. Mga was the last railroad link between Leningrad and the remainder of Russia, the "mainland" as it came to be called. The only way of getting food into Leningrad was across Lake Ladoga and by airlift across German occupied territory. The Germans next concentrated large numbers of tanks and airplanes to the southwest and southeast of Leningrad. In the southwest the Germans, despite desperate Soviet military resistance, broke through to the southern coast of the Gulf of Finland just kilometers (a few miles) west from the city. In the east the Germans made their way to the south bank of Lake Ladoga and seized Shlisselburg, a town located where the Neva River flowed out of the lake. Leningrad was now completely isolated by land from the Russian mainland (See Map 2—Page 28).

In the north Finland had negotiated a military alliance with Germany. The negotiations dated back to a Finnish-German agreement signed in December 1940 which permitted Germany to station troops in Finland, and in the months that followed German troops arrived in Finland in large numbers. Hitler wanted to use Finland as a staging base for Germany's invasion of the Soviet Union in the north. Finland's people knew little about their government's agreement with Germany; however, the great majority approved of their country's pro-German policy. They wanted to recover the territories that Finland had been forced to cede to the Soviet Union in March 1940, and they believed that this could be accomplished with Germany's assistance. By the spring of 1941, the Finnish military had joined Germany's military in planning for the invasion of the Soviet Union. On June 9 the northern Finnish air defense troops, consisting of 30,000 men, were put under German command. On June 17 the general mobilization of Finnish troops was ordered, and four days later Finland's chief of the general staff was informed by his German counterpart that the invasion of the Soviet Union was to begin.

The Finns would join the Germans in a military offensive directed toward Leningrad in June. Finland did not take part in the initial German invasion of the Soviet Union conducted on June 22 because the Finnish government did not think it wise to appear as an aggressor. Three days later, however, when the Soviets bombed Helsinki and other Finnish cities the government of Finland was given the pretext it needed to begin hostilities, and war was declared on the Soviet Union on June 26. In July, the Finnish army began a major offensive in two directions, moving south across the Karelian Isthmus toward Leningrad and penetrating the area located east of Lake Ladoga (See Map 1—Page 27). By the end of August, the Finns had regained the territories that they had lost to the Soviet Union in 1940. Thereafter, they advanced south into the Karelian Isthmus to within some thirty-two kilometers (twenty miles) north and northwest of Leningrad (See Map 2—Page 28). To the east of Lake Ladoga they took control of the Svir River which connects Lake Ladoga and Lake Onega. Leningrad was now encircled by its enemies and more than 2,500,000 people within the city and more than 340,000 people living in the areas surrounding the city were trapped. The blockade around Leningrad marked the beginning of the siege of the city.

Trapped in Leningrad with its citizens were more than one hundred thousand refugees. These people included citizens of the Baltic republics and natives of northern Karelia and Luga and its surrounding regions. They had abandoned everything when they fled from the enemy, either the Germans or the Finns. For many of these people Leningrad was supposed to be a stop over. Upon their arrival they planned to take a train east into the interior of the country but when the Germans captured Mga and then established control over Shlisselburg, the refugees were unable to leave. The refugees hoped that the enemy would soon be driven away and while they waited they lived in crowded and uncomfortable conditions in railroad freight cars. In time, as the weather turned cold, the city authorities moved the refugees to makeshift barracks.

Added to the city's population was a growing number of Soviet soldiers. These men had been wounded in battle fighting for the defense of Leningrad, and they were brought into the city for medical treatment. In order to accommodate the many wounded, the Leningrad Military Council ordered that the number of hospitals within the city be increased. University buildings, the Technological Institute, the Palace of Labor, the Herzen Institute, two large hotels and several other buildings were designated to become temporary hospitals. Conditions were created so that medical treatment could take place quickly and lives could be saved. Citizens would volunteer their services and provide the patients with devoted care. To speed up the recovery of the patients the Leningrad Military Council ordered that they be given extra food rations. After a soldier had fully convalesced, he was discharged and was returned almost immediately to his unit along the military front. Most soldiers, according to the reports, wanted to return to military duty, and their friends were grateful to see them return.

The Germans began shelling the city on September 4, 1941, and two days later they started conducting daylight air raids. On September 8, German airplanes dropped more than 6,000 incendiary bombs causing more than 170 fires in the city. On the same day more than forty high explosive bombs ranging in weight from 250 to 500 kilograms (551 to 1,102 pounds) were dropped on the city. Twelve dwelling places were destroyed, as many as twenty-four people were killed and more than one hundred people were wounded. During the remainder of the month some 2,700 German aircraft were sent to fly over the city but only some 480 penetrated the city's air defenses. Soviet aircraft and anti-aircraft artillery regiments stationed primarily along the western and southwestern outskirts of the city and in virtually every city park and square shot down some 270 German airplanes. Anti-aircraft batteries mounted on Soviet ships in the Gulf of Finland also protected Leningrad. Hundreds of barrage balloons were launched and hovered over the city day and night to further protect the city against low-flying German bombers. All of these developments forced the Germans to fly higher and conduct more of their raids at night. To combat the night raids, search lights were used to penetrate the skies and silhouette the German bombers for the higher flying Soviet aircraft.

Among the enemy's primary targets were Leningrad's industrial enterprises. Before the war began, Leningrad was one of the most important centers for weapons production in the Soviet Union. After the war began, Moscow ordered the city's factories to supply the Soviet military with weapons, ammunition and other supplies and equipment under the slogan "Everything for the Front." The German artillery struck the industrial complexes repeatedly in September. In the explosions many workers were wounded and some were killed. Working conditions in the factories deteriorated dramatically, but industrial production would remain substantial. By the end of the year the Kirov Works had produced 491 tanks, and many of them went directly to the Soviet Forces fighting along the military fronts that were preventing the Germans from entering Leningrad. The weapons factories in the city also produced guns, mortars and shells for the Soviet military forces in other critical regions of the country. In October and November Leningrad delivered to Moscow by way of Lake Ladoga and by air transport vital weapons and ammunition for that city's defense.

Another German target was the Badayev warehouses in the southern area of Leningrad. The warehouses were the largest food storehouses in the city. The wooden buildings were separated from one another by no more than ten meters (33 feet) and when one of the buildings was struck by an incendiary bomb the flames ignited the wooden structure, and the fire then spread from building to building until the entire depot covering 16,188 square meters (4 acres) was engulfed in flames. After the fire was extinguished it was determined that 3,000 tons of flour had been destroyed. The sugar supply, 2,500 tons, had melted and turned into thick syrup with a black crust on top. Later it was made into a hard candy-like substance and sold to the people in that form. The destruction of the Badayev warehouses would reduce the city's food supply, a supply that was already dangerously low.

Preparations had been made in case of enemy air attacks or artillery fire and, they saved many lives and prevented many fires. Thousands of air raid shelters were prepared, and narrow trenches were dug in which people could take shelter during an attack. Workers in factories, schools, institutions of higher learning, social organizations and apartment buildings were recruited for sentry duty. It was the responsibility of the sentries to organize and maintain the air raid shelters. They enforced blackouts in an effort to protect the city from air attacks at night, and they issued air raid warnings. They were also responsible for organizing fire fighting efforts to stop the burning of a building struck by a bomb or shell. Brigades to fight fires in factories and other installations were created, and fire teams to perform the same function in houses and apartment buildings were organized. It was reported that as many as 270,000 men and women were recruited for sentry service in Leningrad's air defense. More than 60,000 people were on duty on the roofs of buildings every night. If a piece of burning shrapnel should land on a roof, the sentry on duty was to extinguish it with water or sand or, using iron tongs, drop it over the side of the building to the ground below.

If the Germans succeeded in entering Leningrad the people were prepared to defend the city street by street and building by building. The city was divided into six sectors corresponding to its six districts, and thousands of people were recruited to construct in their sectors an elaborate system of barricades. The barricades were constructed across streets and avenues between the rows of houses and were made of paving blocks, timbers, railroad iron and steel tubing. They were at least 2.5 meters (7.2 feet) high and 3.5 meters (11.5 feet) deep, massive enough to stop an enemy tank. Anti-tank devices such as pyramid-shaped concrete blocks and hedgehogs were placed throughout each of the city's sectors. Machine-gun pillboxes were placed in the ground floors of corner buildings. Underground communication lines and supply routes were created in the city's sewers. Using the sewers, reinforcements and ammunition could be moved quickly to wherever they were needed in the city. Special points were built into the manholes and sewer openings for directing fire at German tanks and soldiers. In each sector, groups of volunteers were organized to fight the enemy invaders at the barricades, in the streets and from the buildings.

If it became evident that the defense of the city was crumbling, Leningrad was to be destroyed. The Leningrad Military Council had issued tons of explosives that were to be used to blow up every bridge, every large building and every factory. At Izhorsky factory, where artillery shells and Soviet tanks were being made, explosive charges and detonators were placed under the factory's cranes and presses. A cylinder of hydrogen was placed in the factory's reservoir of oil, and at a signal the hydrogen was to be released into the oil which would then cause an enormous explosion.

The methods of defending the city would change after September 12. On this day Stalin ordered Army General Georgi Zhukov to go to Leningrad and replace Marshal Voroshilov as the city's new defense chief. Zhukov had been the Chief of Staff since the beginning of the war and had earned the reputation of being a military trouble shooter. Upon his arrival in Leningrad, he joined Zhdanov and Kuznetsov at Smolny and made it clear that he was willing to sacrifice anybody and anything to defend the city. He issued orders to the commanders along Leningrad's military fronts that a withdrawal would be considered a crime against the homeland. If they should withdraw they would be brought before a military tribunal and shot. Zhukov's deputy, General Ivan Fedyuninsky, told his subordinates "Our principle is this: If you retreat, I will kill you. If I retreat without orders, you will kill me. And Leningrad will not be surrendered."* Zhukov also ordered the commanders to attack, attack and

---

*Harrison Salisbury, The 900 Days: The Siege of Leningrad (New York, 1969, pp. 400–401).

attack again. It made no difference to him if their military units were weak and had few weapons and no ammunition. The commanders who failed to carry out his orders were removed and faced execution. Zhukov's orders were obeyed and by the end of September the enemy's drive on Leningrad had been halted. On the evening of October 6, Zhukov received a telephone call from Stalin at Smolny; he was ordered to return to Moscow. Zhukov handed over his command at Leningrad to General Fedyuninsky.

Having failed to take Leningrad by storm the commanders of Army Group North were given orders to blockade the city, to destroy it by incessant air raids and artillery fire and to starve its citizens. The orders came from Hitler's headquarters and were dated October 7, 1941. Leningrad was to be wiped off the face of the earth. It was reported that this was in keeping with the desires of Germany's allies; the Finns had informed the German leadership that they too had no interest in the future existence of the city. The immediate surrender of Leningrad's citizens was not to be accepted. Refugees from the city were to be driven back by fire if they approached the German lines. It was believed that at least one million people would die from starvation during the winter siege. For Germany this would be advantages because there would be fewer people for the Germans to feed upon the city's surrender in the spring of 1942. Furthermore, the release of the starved citizens into the interior of the Soviet Union in the spring would have a demoralizing influence on the unoccupied Russians.

Already in early September Leningrad was facing a serious food shortage and Stalin responded to the crisis by sending Dmitri Pavlov to the city with orders to institute food conservation and a food rationing program. Pavlov was a civil servant who had devoted his career to food production and distribution. It was Pavlov's responsibility to supply food to the civilians of Leningrad, to the Soviet soldiers along the outskirts of Leningrad defending the city, to the soldiers stationed within the city and to the sailors of the Baltic Fleet. Upon his arrival on September 8, Pavlov ordered his assistants to take inventory of the supplies of food within the city. They counted supplies of grain as well as flour, live cattle and pigs as well as meat in cold stores, and poultry and canned goods. Pavlov concluded that the supplies of grain and flour would last thirty-three days, the supplies of cereals thirty days, the live and dead meat thirty-three days, the fats forty-five days and the sugar and confectionery sixty days. These estimates were alarming, and the city's Party leadership realized that if food was not brought into the city the population would die within two months.

The city's Party leaders believed it was necessary to create a water route across Lake Ladoga and on September 9 the Leningrad Military Council decided to build a harbor in the bay of Osinovets. The bay was on the west bank of Lake Ladoga within a thirty kilometer (19 mile) stretch of land along the lake. The land was occupied by the Soviets and was covered by a thick forest of high pine trees which would conceal warehouses and access roads. The bay was just nineteen kilometers (12 miles) north of the Germans at Shlisselburg and eleven kilometers (7 miles) south of the Finns who controlled the northern shore of Lake Ladoga. Osinovets was located near the end of a narrow gauge railway line, the Ironovsk Railroad, a line that connected the suburbs of Leningrad to the bay, a distance of fifty-five kilometers (34 miles). It was believed that food and other supplies could be brought from the mainland to the eastern shoreline of Lake Ladoga which was still in Soviet hands, an area south of the Svir River. The food and other supplies could be ferried across the lake to the newly constructed harbor at Osinovets. From there the cargo could be taken off the barges and placed on trucks and freight handling carts and be brought from the harbor to the small station at the end of the Irinovsky Railroad line located within the proximity of the bay. From there it could be loaded on railroad cars and transported into Leningrad.

A harbor at the bay of Osinovets was built. The shore at the bay which was sandy, low and sloping was dug out to deepen the draft so that water vessels would not run aground. Army units and workers built four large piers for mooring boats. Warehouses were constructed for the storage of fuel and ammunition and for the temporary storage of food and other supplies as they arrived from the eastern shore of the lake. They were also to be used for the temporary storage of industrial equipment from Leningrad that would be sent across the lake to the eastern shore and to the mainland. A narrow gauge railroad was laid from the wharf to the Irinovsky Railroad line. From Leningrad were brought commercial docks, freight-handling carts for a narrow gauge line and other machinery. Bunkers were dug for various defense purposes.

Toward the middle of September a supply line across Lake Ladoga was in operation. Food and other supplies were transported from the mainland by freight train to Vologda, Cherepovets, Tikhvin, Volkhov and Gastinopolye. At Gastinopolye, a river port on the Volkhov River and nine kilometers (6 miles) south of Volkhov, the cargo was unloaded onto docks and then placed on river barges. The barges were pulled down the river to Novaya Ladoga on the east shore of Lake Ladoga where the Volkhov River emptied into the lake (See Map 3—Page 29). Almost thirty river barges from the backwaters of Novaya Ladoga were brought to the harbor and reconditioned to carry food. On the twelfth of September tug boats pulling two barges carrying 800 tons of wheat arrived at Osinovets unhindered from Novaya Ladoga. News of the initial success of the lake's supply line was encouraging to the Party leadership of Leningrad, but the boost in morale was brief. Three days later five more barges arrived from Novaya Ladoga with three thousand tons of wheat.

Shortly after their arrival, they were spotted by a German reconnaissance plane. Within thirty minutes German dive bombers arrived and sank three of the barges.

From then onward the Germans patrolled the lake route with bombers and shelled the harbors at Osinovets and Novaya Ladoga. In response to Germany's actions, Soviet anti-aircraft guns were mounted at both harbors and the gunboats of the Ladoga Naval Flotilla were ordered to accompany the tug boats pulling the supply barges across the lake. All the barges left the two harbors in darkness. The crossing required on an average sixteen hours and when the barges were halfway across the lake German aircraft flew in to bomb them in daylight. During the last two weeks of September only one tenth of the food that was loaded at Novaya Lodaga arrived at Osinovets. The remainder of the food along with the barges and their crews lay at the bottom of the lake. By the end of the month only 9,800 tons of food had been brought into Leningrad from the east shore of Lake Ladoga. It represented an eight-day food supply for the civilians and soldiers in Leningrad. The city's Party leaders knew that unless greater supplies of food were brought into the city, the people would die from starvation.

On October 12, Pavlov decided to take drastic measures. He ordered 3,000 Party workers to check every ration card. By this time the citizens of Leningrad had been issued ration cards, and now they were required to appear personally with their identity papers and prove that they were the rightful holders. The cards that survived this process were stamped "Reregistered." Those that were not reregistered were confiscated on presentation. As Pavlov suspected, some people were using cards belonging to friends or relatives who had either left Leningrad or who had died. Pavlov's people were also told to look for ration cards that had been forged or that were printed without authority. One woman who worked in a ration-card printing shop was found in possession of one hundred cards and she was immediately shot. Pavlov's measures revealed that more than 300,000 unauthorized ration cards had been in use. Their elimination created a significantly fairer distribution of food and after October 18, ration cards that did not bear the stamp of the Party checkers were invalid.

In early November Lake Ladoga began to freeze, and after it ceased to be navigable Leningrad was supplied only by air. Moscow upon the request of the Leningrad Military Council granted cargo airplanes to be used to transport food into the city, and on November 16 the airlift began. The cargo airplanes were loaded at the airfield at Novaya Ladoga with meat pressed in blocks, smoked foods, canned goods, powdered eggs, condensed milk, lard, butter and other compacted foods. Because of the short flight distance, about one hundred sixty-one kilometers (100 miles), it was possible for an airplane to complete five round trips in one day. However, the frequency of the flights alerted the Germans and they began bombing the airfield at Novaya Ladoga. In response, at least two thirds of the cargo airplanes were transferred to more distant airfields, and from there they continued to bring supplies into Leningrad. These airplanes were only able to complete two flights a day. They were armed with machine guns and would leave the airfields in groups of six or nine. For added protection they would often be escorted by a fighter aircraft. Because there was limited cargo space in the airplanes, the food airlift into Leningrad did not solve the city's food supply problem.

In November the German forces of Army Group North captured the town of Tikhvin. Their mission was to push east across the Volkhov River, capture the railway station at Tikhvin located eighty kilometers (49 miles) east of Volkhov and then advance north and link up with their allies, the Finns, who still controlled the Svir River. If the Germans captured Tikhvin it would sever the last railroad line from Moscow to Lake Ladoga, and if the Germans linked up with the Finns the Leningraders would not be able to use the lake as a route to bring food and other supplies into the city. In early November the Germans, using the cold temperatures to their advantage, crossed frozen streams and rivers and advanced toward Tikhvin. On November 8, during a snow storm, they captured the town. But the freezing temperatures also weakened the German forces and caused their armored vehicles to break down. Even before Tikhvin was taken, the temperature had fallen to -30 degrees Celsius (-20 degrees Fahrenheit). At the same time the Soviet military resistance to the north of Tikhvin was strengthened, and the Germans were unable to continue their advance northward. The Germans would be held in place at Tikhvin for the remainder of November and into the early days of December. They did not link up with the Finns in the north, but they had cut the railroad line between Moscow and Lake Ladoga.

On November 20, 1941, the Leningraders began receiving the lowest bread ration during the entire length of the siege. Workers in priority shops, engineers and technical workers received 250 grams (8.8 ounces) of bread per day, and employees, dependents and children received 125 grams (4.4 ounces) of bread per day. Front line soldiers, naval crews, and flyers and other air force personnel received 500 grams (17.6 ounces) of bread per day. Military men stationed in the city received 300 grams (10.5 ounces) of bread per day. The dark brown bread that was rationed out was 73 percent rye flour. Its other ingredients were 10 percent cellulose, 10 percent cottonseed-oil cake, 3 percent corn flour, 2 percent chaff and 2 percent flour sweepings and dust shaken out of flour sacks. There were other food products to be issued on the ration cards, but during the grimmest days in the winter of 1941–1942, the distribution of these foods was irregular. There were weeks when two-thirds of the population received a daily ration equal to only 500–600 calories.

The authorities sent out search parties to find food and urged experts to come up with food substitutes. Warehouses, grain elevators and freight cars were swept and several tons of flour was reclaimed. Sacks that had been used to hold flour were turned inside out and beaten, and the flour dust was gathered in containers. The sweepings of the floors in a tannery produced leather dust that was mixed with sawdust to make a paste that was added to so-called food patties. In the port of Leningrad 2,000 tons of sheep guts were discovered. The guts were processed into jelly, and the jelly was then flavored with aromatic herbs to disguise the revolting smell. The jelly was then mixed with flax seed and machine oil and supplied to ration card holders as a meat substitute. Any food substitute was considered provided that it could be made digestible and that it contained calories. Botanists pointed out that some common plants were edible. The countryside was scoured for stinging wattles which made a nourishing soup. Branches of young trees were ground up and stewed and then mixed with peat and salt to make a nourishing paste. In time, the workers at the defense enterprises were issued acorn "coffee," kelp casein glue, protein yeast, fermented soy bean milk and other substitutes that would dull the feeling of hunger.

People searched throughout their homes for anything that would give them nourishment. Rats were caught, skinned and roasted or put in stews. Pets such as dogs, cats and birds were eaten as well. The bones of dead animals were stewed for hours on fires fueled with books, letters and pieces of furniture in order to extract a little marrow from them. Books were stripped of their covers, and the glue in the bindings was melted down as an ingredient for soup. Hair oil was used instead of fat. Wallpaper was stripped from the walls, and the residue of dried paste was used as an admixture with flour. The food substitutes were not a solution to the famine-like conditions, and already in November people began to die of hunger which was described as "alimentary dystrophy."

More than fifty thousand people would die from starvation in December of 1941, and in the following month between 3,500 and 4,000 people died from hunger every day. The famished citizens were struck down by death at all times of the day and in various places. They died at midday, while they were asleep at night, by the workbench in the factory or in the street as they were trying to get home. Death in the streets was common and those who saw others collapse could give them no assistance for fear that they might themselves collapse and die. During the winter months the snow would drift over the dead, and their bodies would not be seen again until the spring thaw. The people who died at home were wrapped in blankets, sheets, curtains or rugs by members of the family, tied to a child's sled and pulled through the snow covered streets to a local cemetery. When the living in Leningrad became too weak to pull the dead to a cemetery, civil defense teams drove trucks through the city and picked up the corpses that had been left in the streets, the yards and the city squares. Most of these bodies were taken and buried in mass graves in the cemeteries. Some of the grave sites were long trenches that had been opened with explosives, and the dead bodies were simply tipped into them.

The bodies of the living bore the marks hunger and carried the destructive qualities of deprivation. Many people suffered from heart and lung diseases, nausea and physical weakness, dropsy and scurvy. Their eyes protruded from fleshless sockets, their lips were drawn back from teeth that were embedded in dry gums and their paper-thin skin was pulled tightly over their skull and bones. The stomachs of children were swollen, their heads appeared huge and their arms and legs looked like match sticks. Pubescent girls did not begin menstruating and adult women stopped. Their breasts shriveled. Their sex drive disappeared, and they made no effort to beautify themselves. The eyes of the many who suffered from hunger conveyed an attitude of resignation and indifference. They moved slow and they talked slow. They were aware that death was nearby ready to snatch their lives at any moment, and then suddenly their wasted bodies would become lifeless.

Hunger drove some Leningraders to cannibalism. According to reports, cannibalism was first practiced on those who had died. In the streets, corpses were found that were missing pieces of flesh that had been cut from arms and legs. There were rumors that people were exchanging personal items such as clothing, watches and jewelry for meat patties or sausages that contained human flesh. It was rumored that this was being done at Hay Market, the center of Leningrad's black market activities. There were cases of murder for food by starvation-crazed people. Soldiers, the best fed people in the city, reportedly were killed on their way home from the front. As a measure of protection, the soldiers carried their weapons with them at all times and moved about the city in groups. It was also said that children were beginning to disappear. Boys and girls were easy to seize, and their flesh was tender. Rumors spread that husbands ate their wives, wives ate their husbands and parents ate their children. Stories spread that gangs of well-fed cannibals roamed the city. Anyone who appeared well-fed and looked healthy was under suspicion.

Apart from hunger, the people suffered from a fuel shortage in Leningrad. Both oil and coal supplies were virtually exhausted by the end of September. Cutting the timber that was still available in the blockaded territory slightly eased the fuel problem, but it did not solve it. By the end of October, the city's electric-power supply was only a small fraction of what it had been before the war. In November the tram cars were no longer running. The use of electric light was prohibited everywhere, except at Party offices, civil defense stations and certain other buildings. Because kerosene was no longer available, people would fuel homemade lamps with machine oil, and when daylight turned to darkness they would light a twisted piece of cloth that served as a wick. Central heating in apartment buildings, houses, public offices and factories was stopped. It was replaced by a small stove called a burzhuika which had a small chimney that went out through the small ventilating window of the room in which it was placed. On their way home from work people would visit the city's bombed neighborhoods and take from the vacated buildings pieces of broken doors and other scraps of wood. Many people burned their books and furniture and huddled around their small stoves in an attempt to stay warm. The leg of a chair or table would give a blaze that would last for thirty minutes or longer. People would keep their overcoats on permanently, at the work place, at home and when they went to sleep. Some people would never awaken from their sleep.

The Leningrad Party leaders did all they could to help the people. Thousands of volunteers, despite their own hunger and weakness, were recruited to patrol the streets of the city to find and help others get to their homes or to a hospital. Special "warming up" rooms were organized inside apartment buildings where hot water could be obtained. Infirmaries of a semi-hospital type were opened for the most weakened citizens. The Public Library was kept open and a small reading room in the basement of the building was usually filled with people reading by the light of small oil lamps. Theatres were opened occasionally and actresses and actors gave performances by candlelight or by the illumination of a single electric light bulb. The performers were barely audible through weakness, and most were dressed in their warmest clothes. Many people in the audience fainted from hunger while they watched the performance. For those who were able sit or stand for an hour or two, huddled together with maybe a hundred others, their thoughts were turned away from war and the suffering and death that it was causing.

Assistance was also provided by the Leningrad Komsomol. The youth organization divided its membership into everyday life teams. The teams, consisting mostly of teenaged girls, would visit the people in their cold apartments and offer the kind of assistance that was necessary to keep the people alive. They would chop wood and light the small stoves. They would bring pails of water from the Neva River or from a nearby canal. They would wash some clothes or the floor of an apartment. They would also resettle people into more suitable housing. They placed orphans in children's houses. These were children of parents who had died from hunger or were killed during an air raid or a shelling bombardment. In the Primorski district alone, it was recorded that the members of Komsomol teams visited eighteen hundred apartments in two months, gave care to nearly a thousand persons who were ill and provided assistance to more than seven thousand people.

An organization of ice roads across Lake Ladoga had been in the minds of the Leningrad Military Council ever since the siege of the city had begun. In order to build a proper motor road across the lake, it was essential that the ice covering the lake be at least 200 millimeters (7.9 inches) deep. By the twentieth of November the ice had reached a thickness of 180 millimeters (7.1 inches), and at this time the city had only several days supply of food. Two days later the first motor transport ventured across the lake from Osinovets to a place named Lednevo, located on the eastern shore of the lake (See Map 4 on Page 38). Eight of the ten trucks arrived in Lednevo; the drivers in two trucks had lost their way in a sudden snow squall, and the trucks fell through the thinner ice north of the route. The eight trucks that arrived in Lednevo returned to Osinovets on November 24 with thirty-three tons of supplies. The normal consumption of food in Leningrad was some three thousand tons a day; therefore, the supplies that arrived on November 24 would do little to feed the people. The success of the truck convoy, however, was proof that Lake Ladoga in its southern area could be crossed, and the authorities were encouraged by that.

The drive across Lake Ladoga would be dangerous during the remainder of November. The ice covering the lake was so thin that only small loads could be carried by the two ton trucks that were being used. A system was adopted of tying sledges to the rear end of the trucks and placing half of the cargo on the sledges so as to distribute the cargo's weight and decrease the pressure on the ice. The trucks were also spread wide apart and traveled at a slow speed. Yet there were many casualties. Trucks and drivers were lost. Some of them fell through the ice and disappeared into the icy water. Some were shelled by German artillery fire or destroyed by bombs dropped from German dive bombers. Traffic police were stationed along the ice road from Osinovets to Lednevo, and one of their duties was to lay prefabricated wooden bridges over any holes or cracks in the ice caused by German shelling or bombs. At this time the supply route across the lake was called the Road of Death by those who drove it.

After Tikhvin was captured by the Germans the Leningrad Military Council made plans to construct a road from Lednevo to the railway station at Zaborye located east of Tikhvin. The road was to be more than two hundred kilometers (124 miles) long through forests and across swamplands and small rivers. It was to go through a series of villages—Syasstroi, Karpino, Novinka, Yeremina Gora, Shugozero, Lakhta, Veliki Dvor and Serebryanskaya. Thousands of villagers, men, women and children, were recruited to assist the Soviet soldiers in the construction of the wilderness road. The workers were given picks and shovels to mark the road and handsaws to cut down trees. Army trucks and tractors and occasionally a tank were used to pull down thousands of trees which were laid across the swampy areas of the forests. But the bulk of the work was done by the physical labor of the people. They were fed but very little, and those who collapsed and died from starvation were buried under the wilderness road. Work went on every hour of each day. Makeshift shelters made of branches and tarpaulins were built to house the workers whose turn it was to sleep for a few hours. On December 6 the road reached the end of the forest and was brought across a few farms to its final destination, Zaborye (See Map 4—Page 30).

Within an hour after the road's completion, the first convoy of trucks loaded with supplies left Zaborye for Lednevo. The convoy had been prepared for the journey three days before the road was completed. For the first few kilometers it progressed rapidly across the open farmland, but when it entered the forest it experienced difficulties. The leading truck became stuck in snow. The road was so narrow that the other trucks could not be driven around it, and there was a delay while the leading truck was dug out. The delay was the first of many caused by snow, inadequate construction and enemy fire. The maximum distance that was traveled by the convoy in any day was thirty-two kilometers (20 miles). After six days had passed, the convoy arrived in Lednevo. From there the convoy was to cross Lake Ladoga to Osinovets. It had brought less than a day's supplies needed to feed the people of Leningrad.

The Soviet leadership was convinced that the recapture of the railway station at Tikhvin was necessary for Leningrad's survival. Orders were given to send additional troops to General K. A. Meretskov who commanded the Soviet forces in the Volkhov region. General Meretskov was assigned the objective of liberating Tikhvin, and on December 7 his forces reached the outskirts of Tikhvin. They outnumbered the German forces two to one. On December 9, the German forces withdrew from Tikhvin and made their way westwards to the Volkhov River over roads that were covered with deep snow. As the Germans withdrew, Meretskov's forces took control of Tikhvin, and on the following day began their pursuit of the withdrawing enemy. The campaign to retake Tikhvin was a huge military success for the Soviet Union and an important development for Leningrad. Dimtri Pavlov would later write that the recapture of Tikhvin prevented the starvation of thousands of people and was the "turning point in the defense of the city."*

In January 1942 the temperature dropped causing the ice covering Lake Ladoga to deepen and making it possible to establish more ice roads across the lake. Roads were organized for trucks hauling food and other supplies to Osinovets, and there were roads for trucks returning to the eastern shore of the

---

*Dimitri Pavlov, Leningrad 1941: The Blockade (Chicago, 1965), p. 140.

lake to be loaded with still more supplies. The supplies were brought from mainland Russia by freight trains to the railway station at Tikhvin. Hundreds of workers and soldiers unloaded the trains and placed the supplies on trucks that were driven to either Lednevo or Kabona, a village situated south of Lednevo along the eastern shore of Lake Ladoga. The supplies were then driven across the lake to Osinovets (See Map 5—Page 31). The roads had to be repeatedly cleared and eventually were flanked with walls of snow which helped guide the drivers of the trucks. At each kilometer on the roads stood a traffic guide wearing a white camouflage outfit and holding white and red traffic flags. Communication stations, medical and rescue stations, service stations, feeding stations and combat security stations were also placed strategically along the roads. There were times when as many as 19,000 people were working on the ice roads. "Two trips per driver per day" was a slogan that the more than 250 truck drivers transporting supplies across the lake were encouraged to achieve. To assist them in their difficult work, each driver and traffic controller was given a larger daily ration of food. Before the end of January some fifteen hundred tons of food and other supplies were brought into Leningrad each day. The ice roads that had been established across the lake were saving Leningrad and earned the name the Road of Life.

The ice roads were subjected to almost constant enemy attacks, and Soviet military leaders responded by instituting defense measures to secure Leningrad's Road of Life. Soviet aircraft and anti-aircraft units were used to defend the ice roads from German air attacks. They also defended the roads and railroads adjacent to Lake Ladoga and the bases and warehouses at the harbors on both sides of the lake. The Soviet military fielded some 200 mid-caliber anti-aircraft guns, 50 small-caliber guns, 100 anti-aircraft machine guns and 100 searchlights. Ski patrols were deployed along the approaches to the lake and ice roads to stop German or Finnish diversionary attacks. Along the lake's shores the military stationed rifle units and naval infantry brigades

Food supplies coming into Leningrad would so greatly increase that the city's Party authorities were able to increase the people's daily rations. The first increase took place on the twenty-fifth of December. The workers at the defense plants received 475 grams (16.7 ounces) of bread per day, engineers and technical workers received 350 grams (12.3 ounces) per day and office workers, dependents and children received 200 grams (7.0 ounces). It was not enough to reduce the death rate due to starvation, but it had an important effect on the morale of the people. On January 24, 1942, a second increase in rations provided Leningrad's front-line soldiers with 600 grams (21.1 ounces) of bread per day, soldiers of rear military units received 400 grams (14.1 ounces), engineers and technical workers were given 400 grams (14.1 ounces), office workers received 300 grams (10.5 ounces) and dependents and children got 250 grams

(8.8 ounces). About two weeks later, on February 11, the ration was increased a third time. Special nutrition centers were opened in an effort to help those who suffered the most from the effects of starvation and illness. At the centers the patients were given in high proportions meat and other foods with high protein content, fats, sugar, and cereals. Ironically, hundreds died in the centers while they were being nourished and nursed; their bodies were so ravaged by hunger and disease that they could not be saved.

The Road of Life was also used to evacuate civilians and industrial equipment from Leningrad. In the beginning, the evacuations lacked organization. Thousands of people simply walked across Lake Ladoga and many died before they reached the eastern shore of the lake. On January 22, 1942, the Party authorities made the decision to organize the evacuation of a half a million people. Priority was to be given to women, children, the elderly and the sick. In the month of January more than 11,000 people were evacuated. In February more than 117,000 people were brought across the lake, and at the end of April more than 514,000 people had been transported across the ice roads. When the evacuees reached the eastern shore of the lake they were served soup and other nourishing foods and then taken by trains to the eastern regions of the Soviet Union. Many of them would take up residence in the homes of relatives or friends. At the same time more than 3,600 railroad cars were loaded with dismantled factory equipment and brought from the city to the western shore of Lake Ladoga. There the industrial equipment was placed on trucks that transported the equipment across the ice roads to the east shore of the lake. These items were then transported east and reassembled in newly created industrial plants in the Ural region to produce military hardware for the nation's war effort.

The freezing temperatures that made the Road of Life possible also destroyed Leningrad's water system. For months the Germans had inflicted severe damage on the city's water system, but brigades of specialists checked daily the water mains and made repairs where and whenever they were necessary. In January the temperature dropped so low that the pipes of the city's elaborate water system burst. Fires started by the enemy's incendiary bombs were thereafter extinguished with snow. People were forced to take small pails to the Neva River or to one its tributaries that flowed through the city or to one of the city's canals to acquire water. If a citizen managed to bring home a filled pail and succeeded in carrying it up the ice covered steps of the steep staircase of the apartment building, he or she would have enough water for a few days. The water was used primarily for consumption. Water from the river was clean but the water taken from a canal was dirty and unsafe to drink.

In the spring of 1942 Leningrad's Party authorities recognized that the transport of food and other supplies into the city would be interrupted. The sun and warmth would cause the ice covering Lake Ladoga to thaw, and eventually it would not be able to bear the weight of the supply trucks. At the same time the break up of the ice would create large ice floats which would hinder the use of barges pulled by tugs. The city authorities foresaw this development and so before the warmth of spring weakened the ice of the lake they decided that the railway line from Tikhvin to Voibokalo should be extended some thirty kilometers (18 miles) to the village of Kobona. The railway was extended and thereafter freight trains coming from the mainland could transport their cargo right up to the lake where the supplies were placed on trucks. By shortening each round trip by sixty kilometers (37 miles) it was possible for a driver to make more round trips in one day, and as a result the deliveries of supplies to Osinovets increased. By the time the ice covering the lake began to crack, there were enough supplies in Leningrad's warehouses to feed the people until the spring thaw was complete and Lake Ladoga could be used for water transport. At that time, supplies were again brought by barges pulled by tug boats across the lake. The evacuation of people out of the city would also continue.

The city's Party leadership was concerned that the spring thaw would produce an outbreak of diseases in Leningrad. To avoid an epidemic, Zhdanov issued a decree ordering the mobilization of every able bodied person between the ages of fifteen and sixty years to work on the city's clean-up. Those who worked a full day shift were required to extend each of their work days with two hours of clean-up work. Employees who worked short hour days were expected to contribute eight hours a day toward the clean-up effort. Housewives and students were ordered to contribute six hours of labor a day toward cleaning up the city. Everyone had to carry papers certifying that they had completed their daily required contribution. Newspapers, posters and public address announcements warned that those who avoided doing their civic duty violated the rules of socialist community life and were parasites who were helping the enemy. A person who was found guilty of being a parasite in a civil court was forced to pay a large fine. People who could prove that they had done more than what was required of them were rewarded with a visit to a public bath. At this time public baths were available only to people who were medically certified as being dangerously dirty. The massive clean-up which began at the end of March would last until the middle of April. During the spring clean-up some 16,000 buildings were cleaned, and as many as one million tons of snow, ice and refuse were removed from the streets, alleys, yards, squares, staircases, cellars and sewer wells.

There was also a desire on the part of the Leningrad Party leadership to prepare the city for the upcoming winter. In order to increase the city's food supply, the authorities encouraged the population to plant vegetables wherever possible. It assigned plots of land in almost every park and vacant area in the city. Vegetables were grown in the Marsolo Pole (the Champs de Mars) and in the Summer Gardens, and there were cabbage beds around the sandbagged Bronze Horseman. School children were sent out in parties to the city's surrounding forests to gather pine needles. It was believed that pine needle tea would counteract the effects of a vitamin C deficiency. Wood gathering parties were organized so that no one in Leningrad should be without warmth when the cold winter temperatures arrived. The authorities ordered that all wood buildings not suited for occupancy be torn down and used for fuel.

It was evident that months of air raids, artillery bombardments and hunger had not broken the spirit of the Leningraders. During the siege a sixteen year old girl named Valentina Solovyova described in an essay for her teacher the indomitable attitude of the citizens. She wrote:

> June 22 (1941)! How much that date means to us now! But then it just seemed an ordinary summer day . . . By September the city was encircled. Food supplies from outside had stopped. The last evacuee trains had departed. The people of Leningrad tightened their belts. The streets began to bristle with barricades and anti-tank hedgehogs. Dugouts and firing points—a whole network of them—were springing up around the city.
>
> As in 1919, so now, the great question arose: "Shall Leningrad remain a Soviet city or not?" Leningrad was in danger. But its workers had risen like one man for its defense. Tanks were thundering down the streets. Everywhere men of the civil guard were joining up. . . A cold and terrible winter was approaching. Together with their bombs, enemy planes were dropping leaflets. They (the Germans) said they would raze Leningrad to the ground. They said we would all die from hunger. They thought they would frighten us, but they filled us with renewed strength . . . Leningrad did not let the enemy through its gates! The city was starving, but it lived and worked, and kept on sending to the front more of its sons and daughters. Though knocking at the knees with hunger, our workers went to work in their factories, with the air-raid sirens filling the air with their screams. . .*

Under the terrible conditions of the siege the citizens of Leningrad and the Soviet forces that defended the city would help their country rout the invaders. The first step toward ending the siege of Leningrad began in 1943. Soviet troops broke through the German blockade in the vicinity of Shlisselburg in January. The city, however, would continue to suffer from frequent and intense German shelling; it was not until January 27, 1944, that the German blockade of the city officially ended. For the first time in almost 900

---

*Alexander Werth, Leningrad (London, 1944), pp. 90–91.

days Leningraders could walk in the streets without fearing an air attack. Five months later, on June 9, 1944, the Soviet forces began a major offensive against the Finnish positions on the Karelian Isthmus and in the Lake Ladoga area. On the second day of the offensive, the Soviet forces broke the Finnish lines. By early July the Finns had halted the Russians, but by this time they wanted to end the war. On September 19, 1944, an armistice was signed in Moscow between the Soviet Union and Finland. Eight months later, in May 1945, the Germans surrendered to the Soviet Union. Leningrad's two enemies had been driven off and defeated, and the city had survived a siege that was one of the most costly in human lives in recorded history. Its citizens who had been evacuated during the siege could now return home.

Svetlana Magayeva was just ten years old when the siege of Leningrad began. She and her mother would suffer from but endure the air raids, the shelling, the hunger and the cold temperatures to which all citizens of Leningrad were subjected. These experiences for Svetlana were so painful psychologically, that shortly after the war she repressed them and forgot about them. Years later Svetlana had an accident which hurt her back. The pain that she felt was intense because she had re-injured a wound that she had incurred when a bomb struck a children's house in Leningrad where she was a resident during the siege. The intense pain in her back caused by the accident brought to Svetlana's consciousness the experiences she suffered during the siege. Although Svetlana found it difficult to relive her recollections, she decided to record them so that the acts of heroism, compassion and love demonstrated by human beings under the most terrible conditions would not be forgotten. The following pages record the memories of Svetlana's life behind the blockade during the siege of Leningrad.

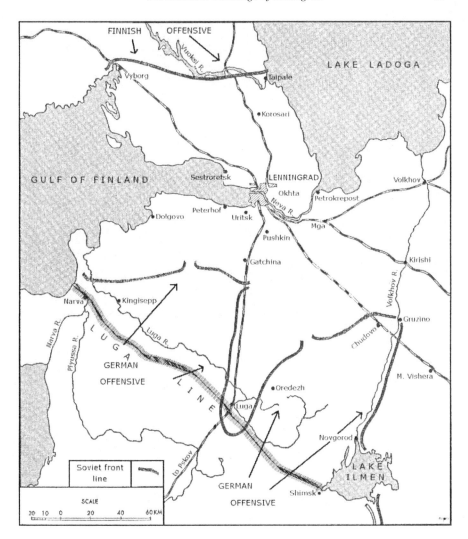

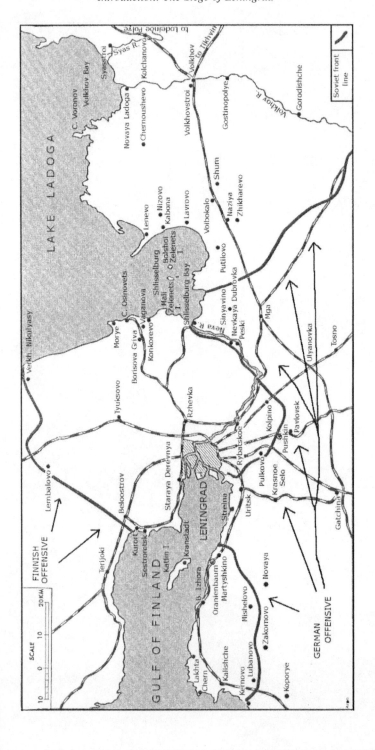

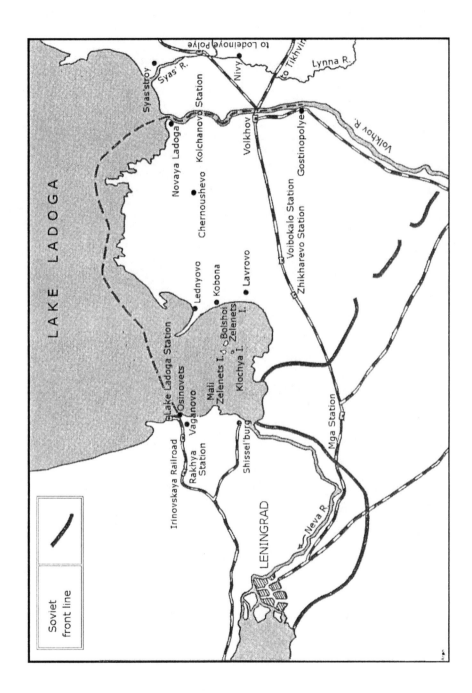

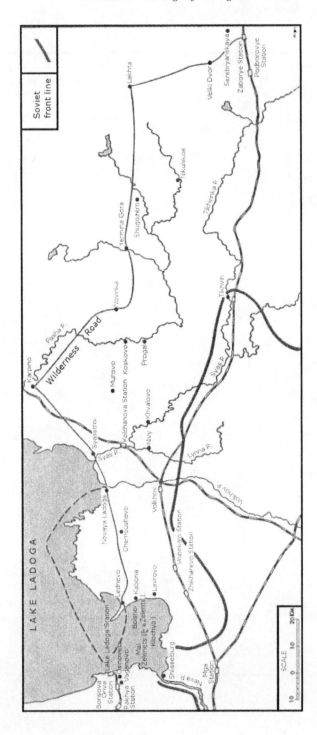

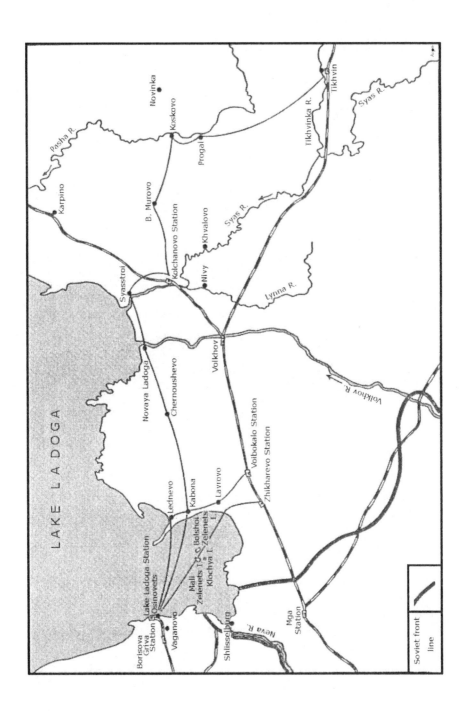

Chapter One

The War Begins

JUNE 22, 1941

A silken blue sky was rare in Leningrad, but June 22 was such a day. It was the beginning of mother's vacation; she was a schoolteacher in the middle grades. She and I had decided to spend this first day of her vacation at Yela-gen Island. The island was popular with the people of our city because it had a recreation park. I hoped we would leave early in the morning, but mother insisted that we spend the morning cleaning our winter coats and the bedding. We were to do this in the back yard of the apartment building in which we lived. The yard was a square clearing about 50 by 30 meters large and was surrounded by apartment buildings that were five stories high. The residents of the four buildings had a special name for the yard; they called it the "well." The name was appropriate since the high walls of the buildings prevented the sun's rays from penetrating the semi-dark area. The yard was to be used by the residents in the apartment buildings, and in the spring the women would use it to hang out and beat the family rugs, winter coats and bedding.

Our neighbor Uncle Vallya helped us carry outside our winter coats and the bedding. He was not a relative, but I called him uncle because he was a close friend of the family. Uncle Vallya also arranged several clothes lines that stretched from one end of the yard to the other. On these lines we arranged our items.

I was impatient to be at the recreation park and complained as we cleaned. I told mother that many people were already at the park. If we had left early that morning I would now be among the trees in the park writing poems that described the beauty of the sun and sky. Mother just laughed. She said that

32

poems describing the beauty of nature had already been written by Vladimir Mayakovsky, a famous poet of the Soviet Union. To emphasize her point, mother recited an excerpt from one of Mayakovsky's poems:

> "The blue silken sky is above me
> I feel well and it has never been so good"

I repeated these lines over and over as I cleaned with a large brush our winter coats and bedding. Meanwhile mother beat the bedding and coats and the sound of each beat bounced off the surrounding walls of the buildings like an echo. I didn't know as I repeated Mayakovsky's words that I would never feel this happy again.

Suddenly Uncle Vallya ran toward us with a look of great concern on his face. He told us that fascist Germany was invading our country. He gave to mother the keys to his apartment and told her that he was going to join the armed services as a volunteer. He then left and headed for the local volunteer office. He was wearing a white summer suit and white shoes made of linen that he had cleaned using white tooth powder.

I was puzzled by the news that Uncle Vallya had brought to mother. I wondered why the Germans were invading our country. The invasion had come so suddenly and so unexpectedly. Yet I remembered being taught that the people of the Soviet Union should always be ready to go to war. I had heard on many occasions people sing a popular song. Its words were:

> If tomorrow a war should come to our country,
> The country will rise up in a moment
> From Moscow to Vladivostok,
> The country will rise up immediately
> It will rise large and strong
> And we will destroy the enemy quickly.

I recited the words silently and thought of the calendar that was hanging on the wall of my bedroom. The calendar bore a picture of a large green tank that had a long gun instead of a nose. We needed such tanks to defend our country. I then recited silently the last lines of the song I had been taught in school.

> On the ground,
> In the sky and on the sea
> Our song is strong and true
> If war comes to our country tomorrow
> If it is necessary to go to war tomorrow
> Then we will be ready to fight today.

The song did not answer the question that continued to run through my mind. Why was Germany invading our country? Yesterday it was reported over the radio that the Soviet Union had sent to Germany a trainload of butter. I told mother that maybe the reports of the invasion were incorrect. I said that I did not understand why Germany would go to war against us after we had sent them butter. Mother did not try to explain. She had a troubled look on her face and told me to stop bothering her with my silly argument. We stopped cleaning and carried the items into our apartment.

After we finished our work, mother and I walked to the school where mother taught. On the way I saw many people in the streets hurrying off to various destinations. Upon our arrival at the schoolyard, we saw teachers and students who had arrived earlier at the yard. Mother's students, who had graduated the day before, clustered around mother and asked her about the invasion. I was pushed aside and found myself standing next to another teacher. He was an old man, and he was looking up at the window of the teacher's lounge. A loudspeaker was being placed in the window. I could see tears in the old man's eyes. I wondered why he was weeping. I had no idea that the war for the people in Leningrad would be long and terrible. I didn't know that hundreds of thousands of people including the old teacher would not survive the war. I tried to consol the old teacher. I told him about the butter that we had sent to Germany, but he replied, "No, Svetlana, the butter means nothing. We are really at war."

When the loudspeaker was turned on we heard the voice of Viacheslav Molotov. He announced that our country had been invaded and that we were at war. He said that we would win the war and that our enemies would be destroyed. He did not say how long the war would last. I expected the war to be over soon, in fact, that same day.

Following Molotov's radio address mother and I returned home to our apartment. For the remainder of the day we waited for the arrival of my cousin Klava. She had just graduated from a medical school so that she could work as a doctor's assistant in a maternity hospital. Mother was concerned about her safety, and she remained awake until Klava arrived. I was tired and went to bed. Before I closed my eyes I asked mother if we would be able to go to Yelagin Island. "After the war," mother replied. As I fell asleep I dreamed about Yelagin Island and its recreation park.

Later that night I was awakened by a whisper. When I opened my eyes I saw Klava standing next to my bed. She was wearing a military field shirt with a wide belt around her waist. On her head was perched a dark blue beret bearing a little red star. I thought it was a dream but then I heard Klava say: "Let's say goodbye. I am leaving to go to the front." It wasn't a dream. Then I heard mother say to Klava "Why are you going? You are a child. You are just eighteen years old." Klava replied that her age would not be a problem for she was going to the front as a volunteer.

Mother and I started to prepare Klava's luggage, but she refused to take almost everything we wanted to give her. She chose a book of poems written by the famous Russian poet Mikhail Lermontov. She also took one of the blue ribbons from my hair and said that it would be her talisman. After that she put her black beret bearing the Red Star on my head. I looked at myself in the mirror and what I saw almost made me laugh. There I stood, just ten years old, in a long white nightgown with disheveled hair wearing a military beret. I looked so funny.

Mother and I walked with Klava to Bolshoy Prospect. It was Leningrad's "white night" season and the first night of the war. I could hear the sound of aircraft some distance away. Klava was in a hurry. So we said our last good-byes. As she walked off she turned and waved. It was almost morning, the beginning of the second day of the war. It was a war that would last almost four years and during that time the people of Leningrad would suffer from hunger, fear, cold, illness, enemy air raids and the death of loved ones.

FOOTNOTE

Klava worked as a doctor's assistant in a military hospital and would travel the roads of war from Leningrad to Berlin. She returned to the Soviet Union in May 1945 with two Orders of the Red Star and many other medals. She also carried inside her a piece of artillery shell that was lodged just below her heart. Klava would die nine months later when surgeons tried to remove the shrapnel.

Chapter Two

Mother

JUNE 1941–JANUARY 1942

During moments of danger mother would become quiet, she would determine what needed to be done and then bravely responded. The children at mother's school loved her and so did her colleagues. I believe they loved her because of the way she conducted herself. She was selfless and always ready to defend others without considering her own welfare. Mother did not like to talk about her adventures or the war. As a teacher she felt responsible for the welfare of her students, and she tried to carry out her responsibilities to the best of her abilities.

Mother was a teacher of biology. I will never forget the first time that mother took me to one of her classes. This was before the war. The class was held in the city's botany garden. Mother's students stood around her and I, being only four years old, sat on the shoulders of one of the tall boys. It was a gray day in autumn, and I remember mother digging up a bush of potatoes. I watched attentively as mother brushed the dirt off the "jolly" young "family" of light colored potatoes and then showed the students the mother potato. She explained to the students that the mother potato looked old and wrinkled because she had given her strength and sustenance to her potato children. The young potatoes had grown strong and were healthy, but the mother had died. Mother then asked her students if they ever thought about the welfare of their mothers. Did they help their mothers in any way? Would they make sure that their mothers did not suffer an early death? Mother warned her students that if they did not assist their mothers then their mothers would become wrinkled and die like the mother potato that she was holding in her hand. I don't know if the students understood the analogy that mother had used, but I remember that it frightened me. For many months after that day I would awaken early in the morning, get up, walk over to mother who was still sleeping and examine her face. Each time I was relieved to discover that mother had not turned into an old potato.

Soon after the war began mother and I were sent to a Young Pioneers' camp. There mother was placed in charge of a large group of children. The camp was located in Valdai, not far from the city of Novgorad. Upon our arrival, the German forces were already making their way toward Novgorad and each day the sound of shelling became louder. Mother wanted to leave and bring the children to Leningrad, but she had not received official orders to do so and so we remained at the camp.

When the sound of shelling indicated that the enemy was fast approaching the camp, mother brought the children to the nearby railway station so that they could be transported to Leningrad. But it was too late. The official at the station said that no more passenger trains would be going to Leningrad. He told mother a military train would be passing through, but it would not stop at the station. We looked toward the railroad crossing and could see that the semaphore was up indicating that a military train would soon be passing through. All the children were aware of the seriousness of the situation, and many looked frightened.

Soon we saw in the distance the smoke of the military train. We could tell by watching the steady stream of smoke pouring from the locomotive that the train was moving at a fast speed. Suddenly mother jumped down from the railway station platform and ran to the middle of the railroad tracks. One of her older students followed her and stood next to her alongside the tracks. They both raised their arms as the speeding train approached. We could hear the train's loud whistle as the conductor inside was warning mother to get out of the way. I tried to run to mother, but someone had wrapped their arms around me and prevented me from joining her. After several seconds but what seemed an eternity to me the conductor applied the brakes. He leaned out the window of the locomotive swinging his arms and shouting. Meanwhile the train's whistle continued to blow loudly. I didn't know what happened to mother and her student as the train which had been slowed went by.

I watched the soldiers in the train jump out of the cars. They grabbed the children and lifted them through the windows and doors of the moving cars and into the arms of other soldiers who had remained in the cars. I must have been lifted into one of the train cars as well; I can't recall. I do remember that my knees were banged up and bleeding, yet I felt no pain. All I could think about was mother. Had she been run over and killed by the train?

I was told later that someone had pulled mother and her student off the railroad tracks and out of the way of the approaching train. The train's speed had been reduced, but it had never stopped. If the conductor had stopped the train, he would have been shot since it was a military train. Mother had also been pulled into one of the moving cars, and she would join me after a while. She then walked up to the officer who was in charge of the train, and together they stood at the entrance of the opened door of our car smoking cigarette after cigarette. Meanwhile the soldiers supplied the children with cans of food and gave them boiled water that had been flavored with sugar.

The train's destination was Leningrad and it moved as fast as an airplane. Sometimes we would see artillery shells explode near the railroad tracks, but none struck the train. The sound of cannonade in the distance behind us became less and less the nearer we moved to Leningrad.

Shortly after we arrived in Leningrad mother participated in evacuating the children of the city. After a group of children had been brought together at mother's school, a bus or truck would arrive to take the children to the railway station. Mother would accompany the children, and upon their safe arrival at the station she would return home. The trip to the railway station was dangerous because the area around the station was constantly being bombed and shelled by the Germans. Mother helped many of the young school children leave the city. I am sure that she could have arranged my evacuation as well, but she believed the war would be over soon. She and I were confident that the Soviet troops would drive the enemy back and out of our country quickly.

In autumn mother and some of her older students left Leningrad to take part in the construction of the so-called Luga defense line. The line was supposed to stop the German advance. Our neighbor agreed to take care of me while mother was gone, but she wondered why mother was being sent out of the city and was being forced to leave behind a ten-year old daughter. I was told later that no one forced mother to go. She volunteered to go in place of another schoolteacher. The schoolteacher's name was Ludmila Ostrovskaya, and she was the mother of two children, a four-year old son and a daughter who was less than twelve months old. Her husband who was a journalist had recently been arrested and condemned as an "enemy of the people." It was not uncommon for the wife and children of an "enemy of the people" to become the recipients of acts of persecution. That is why the director of the school ordered Ludmila to go to the Luga defense line. He hoped that she would refuse to go. If she did, he then would have a legitimate reason to fire her. Mother went instead so that Ludmila could take care of her children. I didn't understand why mother had to leave, and I begged her to stay. Mother became angry and explained that if she didn't go two children would die. "Do you want that to happen?" she asked. "No," I replied.

Before mother left I placed secretly one of my toys in her luggage. The toy was an old rabbit with large ears that had been used in a children's puppet show. Mother would tell me later that the toy rabbit had played an important role. Osip, who was one of mother's students, was a young poet and very witty. He had used the toy rabbit to encourage and cheer up the other students working on the Luga defense line. The toy rabbit in the hands of Osip made fun of Adolph Hitler and said that not even he was afraid of the Germans. But toward the end of the autumn season mother and her students along with the Russian soldiers were forced to retreat from the Luga defense line. During the disorderly retreat the toy rabbit was lost.

Ludmila Ostrovskaya eventually lost her teaching position at the school. By this time it was believed by those who worked with Ludmila that the school director had been given orders to send her to the Luga defense line so that she might be killed. She was after all the wife of an "enemy of the people." After Ludmila lost her position at the school, she and her two children were evacuated from Leningrad. This happened before the Germans were able to establish a blockade around the city. Ludmila and her baby daughter died during their evacuation, but Ludmila's son survived. He would return to Leningrad after the war.

Mother tried to protect me from the destructive effects of fear. She said that there was no need to be afraid. The probability of a bomb falling on us was small. It was much more dangerous to think about death because that could cause a person to go crazy. There was no bomb shelter beneath our apartment building so we remained in our apartment during the air raids. As a result, we did not expend any of our much-needed energy walking or running to a nearby shelter. During the air raids mother and I would occupy ourselves by playing games with the neighbors. The most popular game was lotto. I remember how the tremors of the bombs would cause the glass dishes in the cabinet to rattle, fall and smash to the floor. The small pieces of furniture in the room would slide back and forth across the wood floor. But the adults in the group would continue playing in order to protect me and the other children from fear that would weaken us psychologically.

Chapter Three

Rudi

Rudi was a five-year old boy. He was short and had blond hair, blue eyes and a large head. They said that he was the son of German parents who opposed Hitler's fascist regime. He and his mother moved into our apartment building in the summer before Germany's invasion of Soviet Russia. We were told that Rudi's parents had suffered terrible persecutions in Germany and that is why they left. My backyard friends and I did not understand why such a small boy and his delicate mother would be persecuted. Yet, we knew that they were foreigners because they had difficulty speaking the Russian language and preferred to smile rather than talk.

Rudi and his mother used to walk to the children's playground at the corner of Bolshoy Prospect and the Eighteenth Line. He would be wearing a white Panama hat and brown sandals and would be carrying a small metal pail with a small shovel. The playground included a sandbox, and Rudi loved to build things out of sand. His mother called him Rudi or Rudolph.

Sometimes I would join Rudi and his mother at the playground. I would walk slowly past the playground and when Rudi looked up I would smile at him, and he would smile back. Then he would gesture with his hand for me to play with him. He knew several Russian words, and I was familiar with some German words; we used them to communicate with each other. I would touch his toy bear and say "Die Bar" in German and then I would say "Medvid" (the bear) in Russian. He would look at me and smile and then taking my doll he would ask "Die Puppe?" I answered "kukla" (the doll) in Russian. When a bird flew into the playground, I whispered to Rudi "Die Vogelptichka (bird)" and then together we would laugh. Rudi liked to sing and sometimes we would sing together: "O, Tannenbaum, o, Tannenbaum, wie grun sind deine ecken." It was a winter song, but I did not know any German

40

summer songs. Sometimes Rudi's mother would join us, and we would sing together: "O, mein liber Augustin, Augustin, Augustin. . ." The melody was so melancholy that I couldn't help but feel sorry for dear Augustin even though I did not understand most of the words of the song. But all of that happened before the war.

When the war began the children in the apartment building suddenly were given a freedom that we had never before experienced. Our lives, as a result, would change considerably. Almost all of the fathers and many of the mothers left to go to the war front. The parents who did not join the military, worked in Leningrad's armaments plants or at other plants that produced goods in support of the war effort. Many of the adults worked during the day and would sleep in the factories at night. They would be gone for six days, return to the apartment on the seventh day and then go back to the factory early the following day. While they were gone the old grannies and some older men in the apartment building were supposed to take care of the children. But these people were too old to supervise us. They didn't have the energy, and they let us do as we pleased.

Initially we were happy with the freedom that the war was providing. We would leave our apartments in the morning, come back home at noon to eat lunch and then leave again. We would not come home until nine in the evening. Only the sound of an air raid warning could persuade us to return home earlier.

It was during the period of freedom that I explored a yard behind the apartment buildings. Before the war I had never spent much time in the yard. Stacked against the rear wall of the apartment building that faced the yard were piles of firewood. The floor of the yard consisted of dirt that had been hardened over the years by the trampling feet of hundreds of boys and girls who had used the yard as a playground. There was no grass in the yard. In the middle of the yard stood a Maypole that was named "The Giant's Steps." I was afraid to swing from the pole and always admired the boys who, after getting a running start, would grab the rope attached to the swivel at the top and then fly around the pole.

Leonid was a red-haired boy who had a face that was covered with freckles. He was the oldest of the children that played in the yard, and everyone was afraid of him. Leonid was never mean to me because he liked my light brown hair and the way that I wore my hair. I always braided my hair into two long braids. Leonid did not like Rudi, and on days when Rudi's mother would bring him to the yard she would ask the girls in our group to look after him. Taking care of Rudi involved protecting him from Leonid.

One of the games that we often played was war. One day Leonid decided that because Rudi was German he should play the role of Hitler. Leonid said that even their names were similar. "Hitler is Adolph and Rudi is Rudolf." Rudi did not want to play the role of Hitler and he protested by shaking his big head and yelling, "Nein! Nein!" The girls in the group who felt sorry for Rudi told Leonid that Rudi was not a fascist but an antifascist and that is why, they explained, Rudi and his mother had left Germany. The explanation did not dissuade Leonid. He insisted that since Rudi was the only German in the group, he should play the role of Hitler. Leonid assured us that Rudi had nothing to fear by being Hitler; no one would hurt him.

During the war game Leonid and the other boys attacked Rudi. They pushed Rudi so hard that he fell down, and his nose began to bleed. When I and the other girls tried to protect Rudi, Leonid and his "Red Army" attacked us as well. After the "Red Army" led by its commander had decidedly beaten us, we sat together on the stacks of firewood for a long time weeping. Rudi, who was sitting with us, tried to explain something in between sobs, but he was speaking in German and no one could understand him. Rudi was not angry. His feelings were hurt because others had attacked him with the intention of inflicting pain.

For many days the children of the apartment building were divided into two groups. The girls made up one group. We would play with Rudi and whenever Leonid and his "Red Army" entered the back yard, we would try to run away. But Leonid and his bullies could run faster, and they were determined to hurt poor Rudi. One day Rudi sought protection by hiding behind me. As Leonid and his group approached us, I extended my arms and yelled, "I am a tank! My armor is solid! You cannot get through me and touch Rudi!" Leonid was so surprised at my daring that he left us alone. He and his group moved to the other side of the yard and became involved in some other kind of entertainment. But almost every day for weeks Leonid and his "Red Army" would try to hurt Rudi, and each time I would play the role of tank to protect him.

After a while Rudi and his mother disappeared. We were told that they had moved to another apartment building across from Bolshoy Prospect. It was a large building with beautiful bay windows. Yet it was strong and could withstand the tremors caused by the bombs that were dropped on our city every night. Air raids did not concern us; we were confident that the bombs that were dropped could not destroy our apartment building which appeared so large and strong.

The shelling and bombing of Leningrad provided us with a unique activity. Leonid and the other boys began to collect the fragments of the shells and bombs that struck our neighborhood. After a bombing raid the boys would rush to the area over which the bombs had been dropped and try to find bomb fragments. The person who had the largest collection of fragments was very proud of that fact. Once Leonid picked up a shell fragment that was still hot and the metal burned his fingers. Following that incident, Leonid established a set of rules to which everyone who collected pieces of shells and bombs was required to adhere. According to the rules no one was to approach a fragment that was still hot. After the fragment had cooled, the person who was nearest the fragment was permitted to pick it up and add it to his or her collection.

I remember the day an artillery shell fragment struck the top of a large building located across the street from our apartment building. We heard a terrible explosion, and moments later a fragment of the shell fell to the ground in our backyard. We watched the shell fragment jump several times, then hiss and slowly change color from red to gray. Leonid measured the distance of the shell fragment to each one of us. He found that I was the closest and said that according to the rules the fragment belonged to me. Everyone wanted the fragment, but Leonid insisted that I should have it. "Look," he said to the others, "the war will soon be over and Svetlana does not yet have a fragment. After the war, it will be impossible to find shell fragments so this one belongs to her." I then walked to the fragment and picked it up. It was no larger than the palm of my hand, and its edges glittered. I kept the shell fragment throughout the remainder of the war, but after the war I threw it away. At that time I wanted to get rid of everything that reminded me of war.

A heavy bomb was also dropped on the building where Rudi lived. It destroyed the bay area of Rudi's bedroom causing the windows and brick wall of the bay area to fall to the sidewalk. Many people were killed by the explosion and many were injured. Rudi's mother was not home when it happened and Rudi was not among the killed or the injured. Leonid came to the conclusion that Rudi was in his bedroom at the time the bomb exploded and that the explosion had torn Rudi's body into a thousand pieces. The thought of that happening to Rudi or to any human being was too terrible.

After Rudi's mother returned home she began searching for her son. She went to each neighborhood back yard calling out his name: "Rudi-i-i! Rudi-i-i! Rudi-i-i!" She did this day after day after day. Her voice was loud, and the sound of it was frightening. Each succeeding day she looked worse. She stopped combing her hair so after a while it looked disheveled. She looked at us in a strange way. She had gone mad with grief over the loss of her son. Her appearance and the look in her eyes were more frightening than the bombs that continued to be dropped on our city.

All the children in the apartment building were touched by Rudi's disappearance. They couldn't understand why German adults would kill a German child. Leonid and his "Red Army" went to the kindergarten yard where Rudi used to play in the sand box. There they wept quietly. They no longer wanted to play their game of war anymore. One of the boys wiped away his tears and said, "Soon Russia's airplanes will bomb Berlin and Rudi's death will be avenged." Another boy disagreed. "Why do you want that to happen? Berlin should not be bombed while there are children in the city!"

Leonid decided that we should move all the German children to a Young Pioneer camp. He jumped up and ordered his army to move. His soldiers first rounded up the youngest children in the apartment building and placed them behind the stacks of firewood stored at the yard. Leonid said that these children were the children of Berlin, and the stacks of firewood would shelter them from the bombs that he and his soldiers were going to drop on the Berlin. Then Leonid and his soldiers stood in line to create the fuselage of a make-believe Soviet airplane. They raised their arms to create the wingspans of the airplane and began to drone like the motors of propellers. After that they flew over Berlin and bombed the capitol city of fascist Germany.

In the days that followed Leonid and his "Red Army" would go through the motions of rescuing German children and then bombing German cities. These mock bombing raids would often be interrupted by the German air raids over our own city. During an air raid, we would stop playing and run home. The air raids were becoming more frequent. In the spring of 1942, Leonid would die not during an air raid but from hunger.

Chapter Four

The Bread of Academician Ukhtomsky

OCTOBER 1941

Academician Alexey Ukhtomsky would not leave Leningrad after the invasion of the Soviet Union. He was one of the most important scientists in the Soviet Union. He was also a descendant of an aristocratic family by the name of Ryurich. The family ruled over Russia from 862 till 1598. As a young man Ukhtomsky entered the Moscow Holy Academy and became an ordained priest within the Russian Orthodox Church. At the Moscow Holy Academy he became interested in physiology; it was an interest that would bring him to the experimental laboratory of Russia's famous physiologist, Nikolas Vvedensky. The experiments that were conducted in Vvedensky's laboratory so intrigued Ukhtomsky that he enrolled himself in Leningrad State University and became Professor Vvedensky's most promising student. Later Ukhtomsky became the Soviet Union's leading physiologist.

After Germany invaded the Soviet Union, the political authorities tried to persuade Professor Ukhtomsky to leave Leningrad. He was summoned to "The Great Gray Building," the headquarters of the NKVD in Leningrad, and here pressure was put on him to leave the city. But the famous professor did not want to leave his laboratory for he refused to abandon his students. At the NKVD headquarters he drafted a document stating his refusal to leave Leningrad and signed it "Prince Ukhtomsky."

I was introduced to Professor Ukhtomsky before the war. Mother would talk about him often because she was one of his students. When mother was unable to find someone to take care of me, she would take me to class with her. In class I would sit quietly and watch the old academician lecture.

The last time I saw Professor Ukhtomsky was in the autumn of 1941. He had just left the university canteen where he often ate and was making his way along the long main building of the university. He looked frail. He had difficulty walking. He recognized mother as we approached and was happy to see her. He did not recognize me; it had been six years since I last accompanied mother to Professor Ukhtomsky's class, and I had grown and changed considerably since that time. Nevertheless, he took a small bundle from his pocket and un-wrapped it. Inside the bundle was an academician's ration of brown bread. He divided the bread in half and gave me one of the halves. I refused to take it knowing that his act of generosity could result in his death, but he insisted that I take it saying that the other half was enough to keep alive an old man like himself. He then said goodbye and slowly made his way toward the Neva River. As I watched the professor move away I held the piece of bread he had given me in my hand. I wanted to run after him and give it back but mother told me that returning the piece of bread would only hurt the professor's feelings. When Professor Ukhtomsky disappeared around the corner of the university building, mother sighed and said she was afraid that we would probably not see the professor again. Mother and I shared the academician's gift, eating one small piece at a time during the next two days.

Later, when I was a student at Leningrad State University I studied in the department that had been headed by Professor Ukhtomsky. I would often think about the piece of bread that he gave me in 1941, and I continued to feel guilty that I had accepted it. I related the story to one of Professor Ukhtomsky's descendents. He replied that I should not feel guilty. He explained that in 1942 the famous academician died from sickness, not from starvation.

Chapter Five

Victor Prokhorov

SEPTEMBER–OCTOBER 1941

Victor Prokhorov and I were classmates at the school located along the Thirteenth Line of Vasilyevsky Island in Leningrad. We had shared the same desk ever since our first day of school. Victor had blond hair and wonderful eyes. On a bright day his eyes were blue, and when it began to rain they would turn gray. He had a serious disposition and did not talk much. When he did express himself, he spoke slowly and with a professor's intonation. I considered Victor to be quite boring.

Victor made an effort to be neat, and this was evident in his appearance. Every hair on his head was combed in its proper place. His dark brown suit and vest were always clean and ironed, and the tie that he wore complimented the intelligent look on his face. All the other school children including myself were covered with ink spots. Our fingers, our clothes and even our knees were marked with ink spots, but Victor had none.

The book bag and Victor's pencil case within the bag were the epitome of neatness. Victor always had his textbooks and school notebooks neatly arranged in the bag. The pencils, the ink pens and cleaners and the eraser made of imported India rubber had their own special places in the pencil case. I too owned a required pencil case, but inside my case there existed complete chaos. I always lost pens and pencils, and I almost never had an eraser. Sometimes Victor would give me his eraser with a warning not to lose it. But I would, and whenever Victor discovered that I had lost another eraser he would just sigh. He couldn't comprehend how a person could lose such a valuable item as an eraser; he never lost anything. After a while, Victor decided that he should look after me like a brother takes care of a younger sister. From then on Victor carried in his neatly arranged book bag a second pencil case. If I should happen to lose mine, he would have another one for me.

In September 1941, Victor and I and several other school children continued our studies outside of school. Our school building had been turned into a military hospital and so we were given school lessons at our teacher's apartment. Our teacher's name was Elisabeth Kotz. She would teach us from 10:00 A.M. till 2:00 P.M., and after our lessons Elisabeth would tell us to go home immediately. She warned us that the bombing might begin soon, and she wanted us home and out of harms way. We would then place our notebooks on Elisabeth's dining room table and leave. But on our way home we would walk to our former school's back yard and play "military hospital." Victor never joined us. He went home directly to take care of his grandmother. Victor's parents had left Leningrad to fight along the front lines but before leaving they placed upon Victor the responsibility of caring for the old woman.

During the months of September and October our study group became smaller and smaller. All of us were suffering from a shortage of food, and the pain of hunger made it difficult for us to concentrate on our studies. On days when we expressed a desire to lay down and sleep, Elisabeth would send us home early. She knew that we wanted to learn, but we just did not have the strength to study.

On the last day of our study sessions there were only two students in attendance, a boy and myself. I did not know the boy. I assumed that the boy was from another neighborhood. Elisabeth had us rest on her little sofa after we arrived so that we could regain our strength from the walk to her apartment. It was cold in the room so we did not remove our coats, hats or mittens. Elisabeth looked at us with sympathy and remarked that we had changed since our first day of lessons together. It was difficult to recognize us she said. She told us that this study session would be our last together. She added that from now on we were to stay home and conserve our energy in order to survive the terrible war. She assured us that we would continue our studies in our lovely school after the war.

At the end of our study session the boy and I said goodbye to Elisabeth. She kissed us and said that we had been her best students. It was a wonderful compliment, and I tried to smile in appreciation. I looked at the boy and noticed that he was unable to smile; he had difficulty just standing. Yet he bowed to Elisabeth, took her hand and weakly kissed it. He said that his father had always kissed his mother's hand before going away on a trip.

It was evening and dark outside as we prepared to go down the staircase to the front door of the apartment building. Elisabeth lighted a kerosene lamp and directed the light of the lamp on the steps as we made our way down to the bottom floor. The marble staircase was wide and was decorated with beautifully sculpted designs. The iron handrails were large and felt cold. There was a series of windows that lined the staircase; they were designed to let the light of the sun illuminate the steps during the day. The glass of the windows had been shattered due to the bombing, and the openings had been covered with large sheets of wood. It gave the staircase an eerie atmosphere.

Suddenly I saw the boy sway and almost fall. He sat down slowly on the stairs and leaned against the iron handrails. Elisabeth also saw the boy collapse and ran down the stairs to where he was sitting. She bent down to examine him and turned to me and ordered me to go outside and find someone to help us. I made my way down the rest of the stairs, grabbed hold of the door handle that was shaped like a lion but was unable to open the door. The door was too heavy, and I just did not have the strength to move it. Elisabeth came down the stairs to help me and outside we found a police officer.

The officer walked up the stairs, took the boy in his arms and carried him down the staircase and outside. Large snowflakes fell on the boy's face, but they didn't melt and the boy did not try to remove them. His arm hung downward and swayed back and forth. As the officer turned in the direction of the boy's home, Elisabeth asked for him to wait. She wanted to close her apartment door and walk with us a distance. We waited, and after several minutes Elisabeth returned. We then began walking toward Bolshoy Prospect.

At Bolshoy Prospect Elisabeth took my hand, looked gravely into my eyes and asked me if I had enough strength to walk home alone. I felt sick and knew that I had a fever. Yet, I felt that I should try to walk home without Elisabeth's assistance. I did not want to be an imposition. I assured Elisabeth that I would be fine and that she need not worry about me. Then I asked her if the boy would be alright. Elisabeth looked at me with a strange glance and said that the boy was sleeping. After she helped me cross Bolshoy Prospect she returned to her apartment.

I would not see Elisabeth again until after the war. Shortly after our last study lesson, the authorities took Elisabeth and sent her out of Leningrad. It was discovered that her ancestors were Germans, and those in power did not trust her loyalty to the Soviet Union. After the war was over, the authorities decided that Elisabeth's rehabilitation was complete, and she was allowed to return to Leningrad.

When I learned that Elisabeth had been assigned to teach at one of the schools in the city I went to see her. When we met we embraced each other and wept tears of joy. I asked her if she knew what had happened to my schoolmate Victor. She immediately became serious and asked why I would ask such a question. "Don't you remember," she said, "Victor died after our last lesson together." I was shocked by her statement. "Do you mean," I asked, "that the boy who attended our last study session together was Victor?"

"Yes," Elisabeth nodded. "It was Victor who collapsed on the staircase. It was Victor who the police officer lifted in his arms and carried home." "And what happened to Victor's grandmother?" I asked. "She also died," Elisabeth replied, "but she died before Victor."

After Elisabeth left to rejoin her first grade students, I looked out through one of the school windows and pondered over our conversation. Why did Victor and his grandmother die during the fall of 1941? It is true that at this time in Leningrad people suffered from hunger, but not many died from starvation. Maybe Victor and his grandmother had lost their bread ration cards. Maybe they caught a cold, ran out of firewood to fuel their stove and were unable to keep warm. Is it possible that Elisabeth was wrong? Maybe the boy who died following our last study session was not Victor. I knew that it was unlikely that Elisabeth would make the mistake of misidentification; yet I had difficulty believing that the boy who I had not recognized was Victor.

Chapter Six

Granny Maria

JUNE–DECEMBER, 1941

Maria was not a relative; I adopted her as my grandmother and called her "granny." She was an older woman who lived alone in the building next to ours. I know almost nothing about her past except that as a young lady she had taken the so-called "Bestuzev" which were courses that prepared a person to be a teacher in a special type of school called the gymnasium. As an educator, she had taught courses on the Russian language. Because Maria had worked as a teacher, the authorities of Leningrad asked her to help in the efforts to evacuate the city's 400,000 children after the Germans formed their blockade around the city.

As a little girl I desperately wanted a grandmother. The other children with whom I played had a grandmother, but I did not. I admired grandmothers, these old ladies with their silver colored hair. When they smiled, soft wrinkles would form around their kind eyes. With their quiet voices they would entertain children by telling them fairy tales. After the tales had been told they would serve the children with delicious cakes that they had made especially for the occasion. Grandmothers were never in a hurry. They always stayed home to take care of their grandchildren so that the children would not have to go to kindergarten.

I asked mother to buy me a grandmother. Mother explained that grandmothers were expensive, and she did not have enough money to purchase even the least expensive granny. Besides, mother pointed out, just as adults are required to go to work each day so you too must go to kindergarten and work. She pointed out that I was already a big girl and old enough to work. But at the time I was not yet four years old, and I refused to accept my mother's reasons for not purchasing a grandmother. Almost every day that mother walked me home from kindergarten I would cry, "Oh, mommy! Please earn some money and buy me a grandmother."

On our way home one day I insisted with a loud voice that I had a right to have a grandmother. I then heard a soft voice behind me: "Dear girl, do you really need a grandmother? Would you like for me to be your grandmother?" I turned around, and there was Maria. I recognized her at once. It was as if I had known her for a long time. She had silver colored hair that was partially covered with a white fur hat. Her blue eyes were kind. She carried a white fur muff in her hands, and she was wearing a long skirt.

Maria bent down toward me and repeated her question. "Do you really desire to have a granny?" As her head moved toward mine, I sensed the light fragrance of a French perfume. I stopped crying and threw my arms around Maria's neck. I held her tightly in my embrace for some time because I was afraid that she would change her mind. Mother was dumbfounded by what was happening and apologized to Maria for my strange behavior. But the wonderful old lady was sincere and insisted that she wanted to be my granny.

The next day Maria came to our apartment with some gifts. She gave me beautifully colored pictures of Alexander Pushkin's famous tale about Tsar Saltan. She also gave me a miniature tea set that included cups, saucers, a sugar basin, a teapot and a samovar. The pieces were all packed in a beautifully carved wooden box. The toy dishes were so small that I used tweezers to take them out of the box. I would often set them out just to admire them.

During the war I visited Maria only once. I knew she was busy with the evacuation of the city's children and did not feel right in bothering her. My visit with Maria was not preplanned. I happened to be walking in front of her building when I saw Rudi's mother. She came rushing toward me yelling: "Rudi-i-i, Rudi-i-i!" I was so frightened that I ran into the building and up the stairs to Maria's apartment door. Fortunately, Maria was home and as she opened the door I flung my arms around her neck and began crying. Rudi's mother was still outside of the building, and we could hear her voice through the open window as she continued to cry out "Rudi-i-i, Rudi-i-i."

Maria closed the window to her apartment, sat down beside me and tried to comfort me. With her soft voice Maria told me that the war would soon be over, and there would not be any more bombs or artillery shells. She said that Rudi was probably alive. It is possible, she explained, that the explosive force of the bomb that destroyed Rudi's bedroom had carried Rudi to the roof of a distant building. On that roof, she continued, Rudi had fallen asleep like a little kitten. "Later," she explained, "when he wakes up, he will look for his mother and they will be reunited. After the war is over, Rudi will study in our school, and he will become a fine young man." I knew that what Maria was telling me was impossible, but her story was comforting and I stopped crying.

Maria then led me to her desk and suggested that I spend some time drawing. It was a beautiful desk. It faced the wide windows in the room and was so large that it extended from one wall to the other. Decorations had been carved in its wood, and it had many small drawers that were designed to hold letters, documents, pencils and all sorts of other items.

I sat down in the old armchair at the desk and wrote a poem. The poem was about Rudi and his mother. It was not great literature but it did reflect my emotions, and if the words were recited correctly it sounded like the crying of a child. I don't remember all the stanzas; I recall only the last part of the poem. It read as follows:

> The building continues to stand,
> Only a section has been destroyed,
> Rudi is absent not only among the living,
> He is absent also among the dead,
> An injured neighbor cried out,
> That soon Rudi's mother would die,
> She did not die; she became insane instead,
> She is now walking the streets like a shadow,
> And she continues to call for Rudi.

I was so frightened by what I had written that I gave the poem to Maria. The old teacher silently read the poem. She then walked to her old concert piano, lifted its lid and asked if I would like to listen to some music. It would not be the first time that I watched Maria play. She had played the piano before the war, but the music she had played was children's songs. I told Maria that I would like very much to hear her play. It was serious music that Maria played, music composed by Beethoven, and it instilled within me a feeling of peace.

After the war I found my poem among mother's documents. Written between the lines were Maria's corrections and remarks. I was astonished that the old lady had approached a child's emotions so seriously. Apparently she had studied the poem and considered it important enough to edit and improve it.

The last time I saw Maria was in December 1941. By this time I was so weak physically that I had difficulty standing up and would spend all day every day in bed waiting for mother to come home. On one of these days I remember opening my eyes and seeing Maria looking down at me. She said something to me but I could barely hear her. She repeated herself again and again until I acknowledged what she had said. Maria told me that she had taken some of her personal possessions and exchanged them for a chunk of butter. She then sliced off a portion of the butter, and we shared it. The butter was so delicious. I still remember its flavor.

When mother came home I told her that Maria had visited me and that we had shared some butter. Mother thought I had dreamed Maria's visit but then she saw the remaining piece of butter on the table. Next to it was a note of explanation. It said that Maria and I had eaten our slice of butter and that this was mother's portion. Mother sat down at the table and wept quietly.

At the end of December a young soldier delivered to our apartment some millet wrapped in a small package of paper and several pieces of sugar. He said that these items were for "Svetlana, the granddaughter of Maria." I learned later that the young soldier's name was Peter and that he was one of Maria's former students. He had been given a short leave of absence from the military and used that time to look for his mother. Unable to find his mother, Peter decided to visit his old teacher and leave her the food that he had saved for his mother. Maria had told Peter to bring half of the food to us. She would have brought it herself, but by this time she was too weak physically to walk. Maria wrote a small note to accompany the wealth of food that Peter delivered. She advised mother not to wash the millet so as to avoid losing some of the flour. Mother followed Maria's advice, and in a short while we ate an excellent sweet gruel which mother had cooked on the small iron stove in our dark cold room.

Peter visited us again in the beginning of January 1942. He whispered that Maria had died and that he had carried her body to a place in the city where corpses were to be brought. From there the bodies were brought to a site where they were buried together in large graves. Peter added that he had wrapped Maria's body in a sheet that he had found in her wardrobe. Mother remarked that the sheet was probably made of Dutch linen. The fact that it was made in Holland meant that it was good quality linen. Mother said that Peter had made a good decision, and I could tell that she was pleased. If Maria was to be buried in a common grave, it was important that her body be wrapped in beautiful linen. Before Peter left, he gave us a portion of millet and a piece of bread. He promised to visit us again since we were his only living acquaintances in the city. All his relatives had either died or had disappeared. But we would not see Peter again during the siege or after the war.

Several days after Peter's last visit mother did not return home from her job. I was too weak to do anything so I remained lying in my bed. Someone must have entered our apartment and found me, taken me in her or his arms and carried me to a house for children. The miniature tea set in the beautifully carved wooden box was left on the table in the apartment. I would never see

Maria's gift to me again. I don't know what happened to it. Maybe our neighbors found it and burned the box to give themselves a little bit of warmth. January 27 is the anniversary marking the end of the blockade of Leningrad and on that day each year I think about the tea set that Maria gave to me. I also think about the slice of butter and the handful of millet that she shared with me. Mother used to say that in the scale of nature each seed is important.

Chapter Seven

Kyr Rodin

September–December 1941

Kyr Rodin was a young artist. He was a student at the Academy of Arts in Leningrad and was a talented drawer. Mother and I were first exposed to his talents in the summer of 1941. That summer mother was in charge of a large group of children attending a Young Pioneer camp in Valdai. Kyr's parents lived near the camp and mother took her Young Pioneers to see Kyr's artwork in his parents' home. Kyr's parents called their son "Kyrochka."

I first met Kyrochka after mother and I returned to Leningrad from Valdai. Mother invited him to our apartment. He was tall and handsome and had soft brown hair. The expression on his face changed with each of his movements. He had long thin fingers that constantly were in motion. Their movements were fascinating, and I would watch his fingers as he talked.

During the early months of the war, Kyrochka would complain that fate was preventing him from serving his country. It was not fate but the Academy of Arts that would not allow him to be drafted into the military. The academy guarded its most talented artists through what was called the "untouchable reserved quota." Under this policy gifted students like Kyrochka were not to serve in the military, not even as volunteers. The policy infuriated Kyrochka. He pointed out that there were a number of students at the academy who had been given the opportunity to fight along the front, and some had died to preserve the freedom of the Motherland. Yet he was forced to stay in the rear and out of danger. Kyrochka went to the recruiting office many times trying to persuade the people there to accept him as a volunteer. In December 1941, he finally succeeded. Kyrochka was so happy.

Before leaving for the front, Kyrochka visited mother and me to say good-bye. He burst into our apartment wearing a new military uniform with a small knapsack on his back. It was cold and dark in the living room of our apartment. There was a small fire burning in our small iron stove with its metal chimney. The stove was called a burzhuika and almost every household in Leningrad was furnished with one. We had no running water, and there was no more electricity. But the energy exerted by Kyrochka seemed to fill the room. He was pacing back and forth, and he couldn't stop talking. He proclaimed that he would be gone only a short time. "When I return," he boasted, "we will celebrate our victory."

Kyrochka then placed me on the sofa and began drawing my portrait. He said the portrait would be an important testimony to the heroism demonstrated by all Leningraders during the blockade. Although I was suffering from starvation and felt physically weak, I did my best to sit still because I knew that drawing my portrait was important to Kyrochka. After a while he stopped drawing and put down his work. He said he didn't like the portrait because there was no heroism in my appearance. He said that he would wait until after the war to draw my portrait. I glanced at Kyrochka's drawing and saw an exhausted, pale, sleepy girl wearing a large sweater. Her neck was so thin that it was amazing to me that it was able to hold up the large sized head.

Sitting up to have my portrait drawn drained my strength, and as a consequence I fainted. When I regained consciousness, Kyrochka was gone. There was a full roll of bread and a large piece of sugar on the table. Kyrochka had left the food for us assuring mother that at the front he would get more. Mother and I had an excellent supper that evening, and silently we expressed our gratitude to Kyrochka who had become our friend.

Kyrochka visited our home once more but we were gone. Mother was in the hospital and I was in a children's house. Later, one of our neighbors told us that a young soldier had come by and asked what had happened to us. She said that the soldier had an empty sleeve. The neighbor did not remember if it was the right or the left sleeve. She told the young soldier that she was not sure if mother and I were still alive.

After the war, mother and I received a letter from a professor of the Academy of Arts who was a friend to mother. He wrote that Kir Rodin had been given a great talent, but the war had taken that away and deprived him of the opportunity to be a great artist. He wrote that Kyrochka had always preferred to draw the portraits of children and old people. He used to say that "Children's faces convey innocence and in the faces of the elderly there is no pretense."

Chapter Eight

Misha's Mother

DECEMBER 1941

It was cold in our apartment. Even the stove was cold to the touch. I was lying in bed wearing my warmest clothes with the blankets wrapped around me, yet I was shivering. I was waiting for mother to come home. At that moment someone opened the unlocked door and entered the apartment. It was Misha's mother. I recognized her immediately, and as she moved toward me an overwhelming feeling of fear ran through my body.

Misha was one of the young boys who had been evacuated to the Young Pioneer camp located in Valdai before the Germans established a blockade around Leningrad. Mother was placed in charge of all the young people at the camp, and shortly upon her arrival at the camp she went to the regional center office to get the necessary supplies for the children. Before mother left, she warned the young people that they were to stay away from the nearby lake. After mother's departure almost all the young people walked to the village lake. They took off their clothes, entered the water, and began swimming and playing and laughing and yelling. Nobody noticed that two of the boys, Misha and Vitya (Victor), had drowned. Their drowning was an accident, but mother held herself responsible for their deaths. She would never get over the tragedy.

When Misha's mother entered our apartment I thought that she was going to take vengeance on me for her son's death. It would have been a simple matter. I was too weak to move, and she could have taken a pillow and strangled me. We were alone, and she could leave before mother arrived home. No one would suspect that an act of murder had been committed. Mother would find me dead and conclude that due to my weakened state my heart had simply stopped beating.

Misha's mother approached my bed and sat down next to me. She said she had not come to harm my mother. It was not mother's fault that Misha had drowned, and she did not want mother to live under a burden of guilt. It was the war that killed Misha, she said, and it was the war that should be blamed. These sincere comments should have quieted my fear, but they didn't. I just wanted Misha's mother to leave. Finally, Misha's mother stood up and gave me a hug. She promised that she would give me Misha's bicycle after the war. I responded by saying that it would not be right for me to use it since Misha had died. Misha's mother agreed and then left. I never said a word to mother about the visit.

Mother arrived home late that evening. She was so tired that she did not bother to remove her overcoat. She lay down next to me and almost immediately went to sleep. I remained awake and watched the movement of mother's body as she breathed. In a while I heard mother moan and call out "Misha, Vitya . . . No . . . No. . . ." I wondered why mother was calling out the names of the two boys that night. Had the physical presence of Misha's mother in our apartment caused mother to relive the tragedy that occurred at the Young Pioneer camp? Did mother call out to the boys every night? Once forty-five years later, just before mother died, I was awakened by mother's voice in the middle of the night. She was calling out to Misha and Vitya and telling them not to go out into the deep water.

Chapter Nine

Kamilla Senyikova

DECEMBER 1941

Kamilla was the oldest resident in our seven-floor building. She had two grand daughters, Tamara and Ludmila. These two girls with their mother were evacuated from Leningrad just before the blockade. Their father worked at a factory that produced military equipment, so he was required to stay. He lived at the factory. Thus, Kamilla had to take care of herself. But by the end of autumn she was so weak that she had difficulty standing. The neighbors who knew Kamilla took care of the old woman. They took her ration cards to the nearest food store and purchased bread for her. They prepared meals for her. They busted up her wooden chairs and took her books and burned them in her iron stove so that she would remain warm. Nevertheless, Kamilla continued to grow weaker and weaker.

One day Kamilla asked her neighbors to give her a cup of tea with a little bit of milk. There was no milk available in Leningrad during the blockade. It was explained to Kamilla that there was no milk and that no ration cards had been issued for milk. She was told that milk would not be available until after the blockade. But Kamilla did not understand. Lying in her bed, the old woman with sadness in her voice would continue making her request "Please, give me a small cup of tea with only a spoon of milk." She said that she desired to experience the taste of tea with milk just once more, and then she would pass quietly away. Mother finally promised Kamilla that she would bring her some milk in two or three days. After that the elderly woman stopped repeating her request and lay quietly in her bed.

Kamilla died shortly after mother promised her the milk. We were told later by one of the neighbors that just before Kamilla died, she got out of bed and started looking for crumbs of bread. She took her china dishes out of the cabinet and dropped each one of them on the floor. Then she got down on her hands and knees and began looking for bread among the dishes that lay broken on the floor.

Mother told me that Kamilla had become ill mentally. Her condition, she explained, had been caused by starvation and her desire for food. Mother said that in order to avoid Kamilla's fate, we must not think about food. We should read good books and dwell on the happy experiences of pre-war times. Through these activities, she said, we would remain healthy mentally. I did as mother said and read my old books over and over again. I read Alexander Pushkin's tales, Mark Twain's The Prince and the Pauper and Seton Thompson's Little Savages. I also read mother's books. They included The Etudes of Optimism written by that great Russian scientist Ilya Mechnikov and The Voyage of the Beagle by Charles Darwin. I also enjoyed listening to the radio.

Before the war there were twenty-nine people living on our floor of the apartment building. By 1942 the number of residents on our floor had dropped down to nine. Eleven of our neighbors were fighting along the front, five had been evacuated from the city and four worked and lived at factories that produced items for the country's military. I was ten years old, the youngest of the people who still lived on the floor. Five of us received just 125 grams of bread a day, and the other neighbors received 250 grams of bread daily. Only three of us would survive the blockade. Starvation claimed the lives of many thousands of people in Leningrad during the winter of 1941–1942. The death toll would have been even higher had it not been for the people who through their heroic efforts provided friends and members of their family with food. One such person was Margaret Markova.

Chapter Ten

Margaret Markova

Margaret's mother and baby brother were in need of food. The mother was suffering from a swollen abdomen due to starvation, and the swelling was so great that she was unable to sit. She lay in her bed, kept her eyes closed and did not reply. Margaret's one year-old brother had not eaten for two days. He too had his eyes closed and made no sound. Margaret studied their faces and wondered if they had died. When she saw the weak movements made by their eyelids she knew that they were still alive. She also knew that if they did not get some kind of nourishment soon, they would die. But she had no food to give them. She had tried to get bread using the family's ration cards but when she arrived at the neighborhood bread store, she was told that there was no bread.

Margaret decided to find her father and ask him to help them. Her father was in the military and his division was stationed in the city but on the opposite side of the Neva River. The family apartment was not far from the city's most important river, and if Margaret walked across the ice that covered the river it would shorten her trip to where her father was stationed. She wondered if she was strong enough physically to make it across the snow-covered ice. As she studied the faces of her dying mother and baby brother, she knew that there was no other option; she had to find her father. Margaret was only eleven years old, but the welfare of her mother and brother had become her responsibility.

Margaret gathered her energy and stood up. Suddenly the room began to move back and forth before her eyes. It made her dizzy, and she feared that if she did not lie down she would faint. Margaret did not know how much time had gone by after she regained consciousness, but she could see that it was still light outside so she decided to go.

With much difficulty Margaret opened the door to the apartment, made her way down the stairs of the building and began walking in the direction of the Neva River. When she reached the river she slid down its snowy embankment. The ice that covered the river was blanketed with a thick layer of snow, and Margaret had to lift her legs high with each step as she slowly struggled across the river. Each step was a major effort, and when Margaret reached the opposite side she had to climb up the river's other embankment.

Margaret found her father's division and her father. She did not need to explain to him why she had come. He knew that she had come for food. He could see the shadow of death on her face. The other soldiers recognized it as well, and they immediately gave Margaret some hot water and food. Margaret's father gave to his daughter his portions of bread and salted fish. "Can you get back home alone?" he asked. He couldn't bring her home because he was required to remain at his post at the anti-aircraft battery. "I will try," Margaret replied. He then followed his daughter to the bank of the Neva River. At the embankment he lifted her in his arms and carried her to the river ice. He was not permitted to go any further. "Go!" he said. As Margaret looked up she saw tears in her father's eyes.

Margaret began her journey back to her mother and brother knowing that she had in her possession their lifeline. Making her way through the deep snow as she crossed the river was difficult. Several times Margaret thought that she would lose consciousness. Then she would sit down in the snow and rest until she felt strong enough to continue. She was afraid that if she did lose consciousness, she would freeze to death in the snow. If that should happen, her mother and brother would die as well. She could not let that happen, and Margaret continued to will herself forward.

It was dark when Margaret arrived at the apartment. Upon entering the main room she lighted a home made kerosene lamp and walked over to her mother and brother. They lay motionless, but they were still alive. Margaret lighted the small iron stove, boiled some water and placed the salted fish in the water. Then she tried to awaken her mother by shaking her and talking to her. "Wake up mother," she repeated over and over. "We have bread and even some salted fish." When mother opened her eyes she could hardly believe that what she saw was real. There was food. The lives of two people had been saved through the heroic efforts of Margaret.

Chapter Eleven

The New Year Tree

DECEMBER 1941

It is unbelievable but true; I attended a 1942 New Year celebration. I even received a New Year gift from Father Frost. At the time that I received the gift, I thought that I was dreaming or in a state of delirium caused by hunger. But the gift was not an allusion; it was real. It was a piece of bread along with a sweet stick of glucose. How did this wonderful experience come about?

It happened near the end of December. I was lying in bed waiting for mother to arrive home when I heard a knock on our front door. With great difficulty I got out of bed and opened the door. Standing in the doorway was a young man I didn't recognize. He was covered with snow and smiling. He explained that he was one of mother's students. His name was Dima, and he had come to invite me to a New Year celebration. He said that the festivities were being held at mother's school and that a tree had been brought in and decorated. Father Frost and his Snow Grand-Daughter were waiting for me and that we should leave immediately. I told Dima that I was too weak to go; I didn't have the strength to walk to the Sixth Line.

Dima refused to take no for an answer. He found a small sled in our apartment, wrapped me in a large shawl, took me in his arms and carried me down four flights of stairs to the street outside. He must have placed me on the sled and tied me to it so that I wouldn't fall off. I don't know for certain because I fell asleep in his arms as he carried me down the staircase in the apartment building. I did not awaken until we reached mother's school.

Dima carried me into the large dark concert hall of the school. In the middle of the hall stood the New Year tree decorated with flags and brightly colored balls. There were even some candles within the tree that burned with a weak glow. Dima took off my shawl and had me sit down.

Within minutes a group of people entered the hall and walked toward me. As they approached I recognized two of the people; they were mother's colleagues at the school. It was Uncle Mitya who taught mathematics and Aunt Elizabeth who taught Russian literature and language. Both looked very thin and pale, and I could tell by the way they moved that they were weak physically. They smiled at me and proclaimed that they were Father Frost and his Snow Grand-Daughter (Snequrochka). Uncle Mitya made a good Father Frost because he had such a kind face. He handed me a small wrapped package. I told him that I must be dreaming because what I was experiencing only happens in dreams. Everybody laughed at what I said and applauded. Then Snegurochka, Aunt Elizabeth, officially invited me to the next New Year celebration. They were sure that we would all live to celebrate the start of another New Year.

I was told later that the students in the upper grades of mother's school had organized the New Year celebration. These students helped the teachers look after the younger students. If any of the younger students lost their parents, the older students would bring these children to a children's house, where they would be given food and shelter. The New Year celebration had been organized for these children. It was also organized for children like me who no longer attended school because we were too weak to do so. That is why Dima had come to the apartment.

Following the New Year celebration Dima brought me home. Again he wrapped me in my shawl and tied me to the sled. On the way I fell asleep, and when I woke up I was home. As my eyes searched the room I saw the package that Father Frost had given me. Mother smiled and assured me that I was not dreaming. I had truly attended a New Year celebration and Uncle Mitya and Aunt Elizabeth had played the parts of Father Frost and Snegurochka. I believe that this was their last New Year celebration because both teachers died during the blockade.

I remember distinctly how mother and I welcomed in the New Year. She awakened me just before midnight. There was a fire burning in our small iron stove. Mother had placed the dinner table next to our bed. Our small kerosene lamp created an arch of light over the top of the table and illuminated a large bottle of champagne. Next to the bottle was a plate holding scones that had been made with coffee grounds. It was fantastic. Mother explained that she had purchased the champagne with the ration cards that she had not been able to use. Since December 27 the food store where mother purchased our bread had no bread to sell. So mother used our ration cards to purchase the champagne. After we drank the champagne and ate the scones we turned on the radio. We listened to the chiming of the bells at Red Square in Moscow, and we listened to the voices of Leningrad poets who congratulated the city's people on a new year. Mother and I believed strongly that Leningrad would survive the blockade.

Chapter Twelve

The Disappearance of Mother

JANUARY 11, 1942

It was in early January that I became ill from starvation. I was so weak that I barely had enough strength to stand. I wanted to sleep, but I couldn't. The constant pangs of hunger in my stomach kept me awake. So I would lie in bed in my winter overcoat under several blankets. I kept my hands in my granny's soft white fur muff. The muff not only warmed my hands but it also brought to mind the wonderful memories that I had of my adopted grandmother. That warmed my soul. All day long I would wait for mother to come home. I would hear the explosions of German bombs and shells, but they did not frighten me anymore. What I feared was losing mother. I wanted her home. She was everything to me, and I could not imagine what life would be like for me without her. She loved me, and I felt secure in her presence.

After the war mother told one of her close friends that during the terrible hunger of January, 1942, I would give mother small pieces of my portions of bread. She said that I would do this after she had turned her back toward me. I don't remember doing this, but it is very possible that I did try to give mother some of my daily portion of bread. I am sure that I believed she needed and deserved a larger portion than me. I was told this story by my mother's friend a month after mother died. She further told me that mother was aware that I was trying to give her pieces of my bread, but when I was not looking she would return my pieces and add to them some of her own portion. She added that my love for mother helped her endure the hardships that we suffered as a result of the blockade.

In January mother and some of her colleagues were given a war assignment. They were to search the apartment buildings of their school neighborhood in search of children who had become orphaned due to the deaths of their parents. Each day the teachers would climb the ice covered stairs of the buildings in search of children that were living alone in the apartments. In almost every apartment they witnessed the horrible effects of the blockade. They saw people, both adults and children, lying in their beds too weak to move and suffering from starvation. They found people who were lying dead in their beds. If a child was found who was still alive and alone, the child was to be taken to a children's house.

One day mother slipped on the icy staircase of an apartment building that she had searched. She fell to the floor and couldn't get up. Mother was too weak from starvation. Had she laid there for more than an hour, she would have died from the cold. Fortunately, some of mother's students found her shortly after she fell. They carried her to the hospital located on the Fifteenth Line and had mother admitted as a patient. Mother's condition was declared critical. I knew nothing about mother's accident. All I knew was that mother did not arrive home that evening. It was January 11, 1942.

Chapter Thirteen

Jan Tissler

JANUARY 1942

After mother was hospitalized there were just Uncle Jan and myself living on the fourth floor of our apartment building. Uncle Jan was suffering from starvation. Early in January he had returned home from the Baltic Ship Production Mills where he worked as a mechanic. The trip home must have been too hard on him because after he entered his room he lay down and would not get up again.

Since the beginning of the war Uncle Jan had returned home from the mills just once a week. But each week, our tall strong neighbor would walk slower and move around with greater difficulty. His feet began to swell due to starvation, and walking became a painful experience. There were weeks when he was too tired to take off his coat after he arrived home. He would drop his body on the sofa and fall asleep. Sometimes mother and I would enter his apartment to see how he was doing. If we found him sleeping in a seated position, we would lift his heavy swollen feet on the sofa so that he would rest more comfortably. We would stand by the sofa and watch him for a while. Then we would leave. Uncle Jan would stay on the sofa until it was time to return to the mills.

The time came when mother found Uncle Jan in a collapsed position near the bottom of the staircase of our building. He told mother he was unable to climb the stairs. He tried several times, but each time he had fainted. Mother wanted to take him to a nearby hospital, but Uncle Jan refused to go. Mother then helped Uncle Jan into his apartment and into bed.

On the day that mother did not return home I unlocked the door of our apartment and opened it just a little. I was hoping that someone would enter

68

the apartment building and find me. Uncle Jan was married but his wife worked as a fire fighter, and she rarely came home. It would have to be someone like mother whose job it was to search apartment buildings for abandoned children. After climbing back in bed I fell asleep. It was no longer difficult to sleep because the hunger pangs had stopped. I was no longer feeling anything.

The next morning a teacher from another neighborhood school came to our building looking for orphans. She found me lying in bed, and together we entered Uncle Jan's apartment. We found him lying dead in his bed. We stood near the bed for a while, and I wept quietly. The teacher then covered Uncle Jan's face with the bed sheet and took off his slippers and placed them under the bed. Before the war I would often play with those slippers. I would take one of the slippers and pretend that it was a ship. It was so large that I could fit two of my dolls in the slipper and take the dolls on a trip to a faraway land. Those times before the war were happier times.

The teacher who had found me was in a hurry. In January in Leningrad it turns dark early. She told me that she was going to bring me to a children's house, and she wanted to get there before it turned dark. She bundled me up, carried me down the stairs and held my hand as we walked along the snow covered streets. On the way I would periodically lose consciousness. Finally, the teacher, who was suffering from starvation, took me in her arms and carried me the rest of the way. Her swollen feet made every step that she took painful.

Chapter Fourteen

The Children's Houses

The lives of thousands of children were saved in the children's houses in Leningrad during the winter of 1941–1942. Even during the most difficult days when there was little food in the city, the children in the children's houses were fed. They were given bread three times a day and warm gruel two times a day. Twice a day they were given a cup of hot tea. On days when it was available the children would receive a piece of sugar or a small slice of butter.

There were two types of children's houses in Leningrad; one was a distribution house and the other was a stationary house. At a distribution house the doctors would examine each child brought to the house and decide if the child should stay or be sent to a stationary house. A child who suffered from dysentery was sent to a stationary house which was a hospital for patients with infections. A child who was diagnosed with tuberculosis was sent to a stationary house in which patients suffering from tuberculosis received care.

When a sense of feeling returned to a child who had been brought to a distribution house and the child regained the ability to move the child was moved to a stationary children's house. Children who were cared for in a stationary children's house were prepared for their eventual evacuation from Leningrad. The children who were evacuated were brought out of the city by train to the western shore of Lake Ladoga. Then they were placed on trucks (in the winter months) or on boats (in the spring and summer months) and brought across the lake. After reaching the opposite shore they were placed on trains and brought east as far as the Ural Mountains and Asia. The evacuation was difficult and dangerous. German aircraft would attack the trucks and trains, in spite of the fact that the trains bore the emblem of "The Red Cross." In the meantime, the beds in the stationary children's houses that had been used by the children who were being evacuated were immediately occupied by Leningrad's new orphans.

Chapter Fifteen

Going to see Mother

JANUARY 1942

In January I was brought to a distribution children's house. I remember almost nothing about my stay in that house. I slept all day and all night long from one meal to the next. It was cold in the building, and all the children lay in bed with their coats on. We ate our meals and drank our hot tea quietly. I do not know why, how or when it happened but shortly after I was admitted to the distribution children's house, I learned about my mother's whereabouts.

At the distribution children's house I was awakened whenever I was brought something to eat or drink. One day I was awakened at an unusual time. Bending over me was a young lady wearing a padded jacket and a hat with earflaps. She was a former student of mother and was one of several students who had carried her to the hospital after finding her lying near the staircase of an apartment building. The young lady told me that mother was in a coma when she was admitted to the hospital and had not regained consciousness. She said that she and others were taking care of mother and had been trying to bring her out of her coma. Mother would say only the name "Svetlana," and she would repeat it again and again. Mother's students then went searching for me, but they found our apartment empty. They were told that I had been taken to a children's house. At that time there was only one children's house in our district and so this former student of mother found me at once. Before leaving she promised that she would return to visit me, but I would not see her again.

Mother was alive, and I wanted to see her. I slipped out of my bed and quietly moved out of the room and down the stairs of the children's house. The front door was large and heavy, but after much effort I finally managed to

71

open it. Opening the door was so exhausting that I was forced to sit on a mound of snow near the door to regain my strength. When I felt strong enough I got up and moved slowly along a narrow path in the deep snow that covered the sidewalk. After a while I fell down, laid there on the snow packed path for a minute or two and got up to continue my difficult journey to mother. But I would fall again and again until at last I did not have the strength to get up. I then rolled onto my side, and with my legs and feet I pushed my body forward on the snow. In time a soldier crossed my path and asked me where I was going. I told him I was going to see my mother who was in the hospital on the Fifteenth Line. He took me in his arms and carried me to the hospital.

I hardly recognized mother. The skin of her face was ashen pale. She had no hair. Her head had been shaved so she would not suffer from lice. She had difficulty seeing, and when I spoke to her she did not seem to understand what I was saying. Poor mother didn't even recognize me.

A lady in a white doctor's smock suddenly appeared and introduced herself. Her name was Klaudia, and I assumed that she was the director of the hospital. She told me that mother was suffering from the severest case of dystrophy. She believed that it would take a long time for mother to recover fully from the illness. Klaudia explained that while mother was lying unconscious in the snow one of her feet froze, and she feared that it might be necessary to amputate it.

I tried to visit mother everyday. I would leave the children's house right after breakfast. I would set aside a portion of my breakfast and place it in a small cup. It was several spoons of liquid soup made with flour and several small pieces of bread. The pieces of bread would soak up the soup. After placing the cup in my mitten, I left the children's house to visit mother. The winter of 1941–1942 was particularly cold, yet I didn't feel cold in spite of the fact that there were holes in my mittens. Maybe I had already entered a level of dystrophy where a person loses the sense of feeling.

When I reached the hospital several blocks away I had to wait at the entrance for someone to open the door. The large door was too heavy for me to open. So I would sit on the top step of the building's steps and wait for someone to walk by. Waiting was difficult for I desired to see mother. Often a soldier would walk by, and he would open the heavy door for me.

After I entered the hospital I had to climb a flight of stairs to mother's ward on the second floor of the building. Getting to the top of the stairs was a long and cumbersome process for I was too weak to climb the stairs standing up. I began the process by sitting down on the second step with my back facing the top of the stairs. Then with my hands I lifted my feet onto the first step. Then I placed my hands on the second step, and with my arms I would push myself up and sit on the third step. With my hands I then lifted my feet onto the second step. When I reached the top, I would stand up and make my way to mother's room. Her bed had been placed to right side of the door. She would lie motionless, but when I touched her lips with my spoon she opened her mouth and I would feed her the bread and soup. I would stay for only a short while because I had to return to the children's house before dinner, and the trip back took me a long time.

Doctor Klaudia did not like for me to bring food to mother. She was concerned about my health and wanted me to eat all the food that was given to me at the children's house. At the children's house I was given dinner and supper every day as well as a daily concoction of pine needles that was rich in vitamins. The food that I received made me feel strong enough to visit mother everyday. It seemed to me that mother looked worse with each visit, and I believed my little cup of bread with soup would save her.

One day I arrived at the hospital with a piece of bread that a military officer had given me. He saw me making my way to the hospital, lifted me in his arms and carried me the rest of the way. He then gave me a piece of bread and told me to eat it because it would give me strength. I wanted to give the bread to mother, but when I reached the second floor of the hospital building I heard the angry voice of Doctor Klaudia. She ordered someone to "tell that girl that her mother has died, and she is not to come to hospital again." I was so shocked at what I heard that I jumped up from the stairs and rushed to mother's room. Mother was lying in her usual position, and she was breathing. I then started to cry hysterically.

Some of the hospital attendants took me out of mother's room and brought me to Doctor Klaudia. She said that she was sorry that she had ordered someone to tell me that mother had died. She explained that she felt the lie was necessary. If I continued to visit mother each day in order to feed her I would eventually kill myself. If I believed that mother was dead, I would stop making the depleting daily trips to the hospital. But I wasn't listening to Doctor Klaudia; I was in a state of hysteria. The attendants gave me some medicine and then brought me back to the distribution children's house. For days after this I was too weak to get up. I just lay in bed and wondered if mother was still alive.

Chapter Sixteen

Winter in the Children's House

WINTER 1941–1942

During my stay at the stationary children's house I came to know many people. Some were caring, comforting and loving toward others and some were indifferent, hostile and hurtful. All of the children were ill due to hunger. Many suffered from physical ailments such as dystrophy and severe diarrhea as well as from anxiety and depression. A large percentage of the children died in spite of the care that they received from the doctors and the teachers who had been assigned to watch over us. The children who survived the winter months of 1941–1942 and became strong enough physically to be evacuated out of Leningrad would leave the children's house in the summer and the autumn of 1942. This chapter and the chapters that follow are devoted to the adults who worked in the children's house and to the children who were my companions in the house.

MARK (MARICK) AND ALEXANDER (SASHA) ALTSHOOLERS

Marik was the youngest child in our room. He was not even two years old and he was so small that he looked like a baby. Marik had come to the children's house with his brother Sasha who was much older. Sasha occupied a bed in another room where the teenagers were kept.

Marik would never lie still and was constantly moaning and crying. The teachers in the children's house tried to get him to stop crying but they were unsuccessful. One of the children in the room, Alik Nesterov, who was not much older than two, also tried to quiet Marik. Alik slipped out and down

74

from his bed, walked over to Marik and asked him why he was crying. He asked Marik if there was something he could do to help. Marik did not answer; he continued crying. Alik then threw up his hands, shrugged his shoulders and returned to his bed.

After a while Sasha entered our room. Someone had told him that his brother was crying and asked him to find out what was wrong. Sasha was suffering from dystrophy and had difficulty keeping his balance. He held on to the frames of the beds as he made his way to his little brother's bed. Sasha knew what Marik wanted as he sat down next to him. Sasha pulled off his sweater and began unbuttoning his shirt. As he did we could see the protruding bones of his rib cage and the outline of his collarbone. Sasha took Marik in his arms and carefully pressed his brother's small head against his chest. "Don't cry Marik," he said with a soft voice, "Mommy will be here soon but in the meantime I will sing you a song." Marik did not wait for Sasha to begin singing. He found "mother's" nipple and began sucking. Almost immediately Marik fell asleep. Sasha then laid his brother back in bed, covered him with a blanket and left the way he had come.

Whenever Marik awakened he would begin crying, and he would continue crying until Sasha gave him his nipple. Sasha's nipple pacified Marik, and when the little boy went to sleep the room became silent. It was difficult for Sasha to walk from his room to ours and then back to his room, and doing this several times a day sapped his strength. So the teachers at the children's house decided to move Marik into Sasha's room.

TATIANA (TANYA) UTKINA

Tanya was eight years old and suffered from a severe case of diarrhea. She looked like a living mummy. She had the face of an old woman. Her arms and legs were as thin as spaghetti noodles. The doctor tried to inject Tanya with glucose, but her body was so dehydrated that the doctor had great difficulty giving her an injection. Tanya knew that her body was dying, yet she desperately desired to live.

One of the teachers at the children's house did everything within her power to keep Tanya alive. She would wash Tanya several times a day. She would change her bed sheets each time that Tanya had an accident. There were nights when she would sit by Tanya's bed in case her assistance was needed. In the morning the teacher would tell Tanya that she looked healthier than the day before. She said this to encourage Tanya, and it did.

The children in the room also tried to encourage Tanya. Often Tanya would ask if we thought she was going to die, and we replied of course not. We assured her that she would be better soon and that after she regained her strength she would again run and jump and play.

The impossible dream came true. The diarrhea stopped, and Tanya gained weight. After a while she could stand up and walk. The children in the room and the adults in the children's house gathered around Tanya to watch her walk. They witnessed a miracle. Tanya smiled as she took one step after another. She joked that she should demand a fee from each of us for her demonstration. Tanya's recovery was an encouragement to others in our room. They believed that if Tanya was able to recover from severe diarrhea, they certainly were able to survive dystrophy and the war.

Towards the end of the war a kind hearted lady arrived at the children's house requesting permission to adopt Tanya. The lady had already adopted Tanya's baby sister. Tanya and her sister had been separated from each other after they became orphans. But Tanya discovered that the lady had a son, and he did not want to share his mother with other children. As a result, Tanya told the lady she did not want to be adopted. Tanya would remain living in the children's house until the war ended.

EDWARD (ADICK) DERJUGIN

Adick had become a war orphan on New Years Day, 1942. His mother who worked at a local factory arrived home from work early one day. At 10:00 A.M. she died. Adick was nine years old. The death of his mother had such a devastating effect on Adick that he would never again celebrate the arrival of a new year.

Taking care of himself and providing for his younger brother was now Adick's responsibility. He did not know what to do with the body of his mother. He had no fire wood to burn in their iron stove, and the temperature within the apartment dropped dramatically. There was nothing to eat so the brothers lay quietly in bed for six days. During that time no one came to the apartment in search of mother or in search of her orphans.

On the seventh day after his mother's death Adick decided to go for help. He realized that if his brother, Tolya, and he did not eat soon they would die. Adick slid out and down the side of his bed and slowly made his way out the apartment door and to the nearby factory where his mother had worked. The director of the factory recognized Adick immediately and had someone carry Adick back to the apartment. For the next three weeks the director had one of his female workers bring the brothers two cups of soup everyday.

During those weeks the supervisor of the apartment building where Adick and his brother lived became the self-proclaimed guardian of the two orphans.

He used their bread ration cards and their other ration cards to acquire food. He gave a small portion of the food to the brothers, but the majority he would use to better feed himself. Using another person's ration card was a crime, and the supervisor knew that. When the boys became ill from starvation, the supervisor brought them to our children's house.

It was toward the end of January 1942, when Adick and Tolya were brought into our children's house. By this time they were severly ill due to starvation, and they were sent immediately by the doctor at the children's house to a nearby hospital. Tolya never recovered from his illness. His death could have been avoided if the apartment supervisor had brought them to the children's house immediately.

Adick was tall and handsome. He had dark auburn colored hair. He had a "foreign" nose. He was my age, but intellectually he was two years older. He was a wonder child. He had not invented something and he had not discovered a new law in physics, but it was evident that he had the potential of doing so. Others would approach him and expect from him some clever saying and some brilliant solution to a problem. These expectations were hard on Adick. He was also well behaved. He never participated in mischievous activities and would condemn prankish acts committed by others in the room. The teachers noticed quickly that Adick was responsible, and they would place him in charge of monitoring us when they were absent from the room. Thus he became our leader and would become an assistant to our teachers. He carried upon his shoulders the cares and responsibilities meant for an adult. He rarely smiled and tried to be serious at all times and was often stern in his attitude.

Adick became a nurse to many of the children in our room. He made sure that our needs were met and that was especially true of the youngest children. When clothes were donated to the children's house, Adick distributed the clothes making sure that each child received clothes and that they were not too small or large. One day Lisa and Vera confided in Adick that their underwear was too small. They had been wearing the same underwear for a couple of years, and they had grown out of it. They knew Adick would not think this was humorous and that he would not joke about their problems. Adick helped the two sisters get underwear that was more comfortable to wear.

Derjugin was Adick's last name, but this became known to us only after he shared with us a family secret. Adick was a private individual and did not talk about his past. It was during a rare moment that he told me that his father was a German, and his mother was Russian. His father's last name was Lerner, and after the war broke out life for people with last names that were German became more difficult. They were viewed with suspicion, some were ostracized and a number of them were attacked verbally and physically.

In order to safeguard her sons, Adick's mother gave them her maiden name which was Derjugin. She also gave Adick a middle name, Valentine; her name was Valentina. Both Derjugin and Valentine were Russian names. Adick's full name became Adick Valentine Derjugin. After Adick shared this information with a few of us we vowed that we would keep it a secret, and thereafter we became like family.

NAMELESS CHILDREN

There were some children whose names were not known. They were orphans whose fathers had been called into the military and whose mothers had died. They were usually found in their parents' apartment, and most if not all were suffering from starvation. When they were carried into the children's house and laid to rest on a bed, they would not move or make a sound. They were barely breathing. They were not sleeping. They were unconscious. When a spoon of food touched their lips, their lips would move and take the food into their mouths. They then swallowed with great difficulty. Not one of these children survived, not one. They died soundless and nameless.

Chapter Seventeen

Doctor Lyolya

WINTER 1941–1942

Doctor Lyolya was sent to our children's house by the Medical University in Leningrad. She arrived during the winter of 1942. She was exhausted and pale; she had blond hair and a nice warm voice. She came into our room every morning to examine us. If she found that someone had died during the night she would leave the room and return shortly thereafter with a stretcher and an assistant. She and her assistant would then lift the dead child onto the stretcher and carry the body upstairs in a room directly above our room. There the child's body was stored along with all of the other children who had died. In the spring the corpses were removed and taken by a special group of soldiers to the Smolensk cemetery to be buried. We knew that the room above us was used to store the corpses, but their presence never frightened us.

In the beginning we did not like Doctor Lyolya. We saw her as the herald of death. She was a physician, but she did not have the medicines to treat a person who was dying from starvation. I could tell that she suffered from the inability to help us. She wore a military uniform, and with her assignment came responsibilities. She carried out her responsibilities faithfully, and in time we recognized the necessity and importance of her assignment.

Every morning Doctor Lyolya examined each child within our large room. If a child did not move, she would take out a small mirror and place it up to the child's nose. If the mirror became fogged, Doctor Lyolya knew the child was still breathing if ever so slightly. All of us were familiar with the procedure, and we took special notice whenever Doctor Lyolya took out her small mirror.

One morning the little mirror was placed against my nose. It was Doctor Lyolya's nurse who carried out the procedure, and she called in Doctor

Lyolya after she noticed that the mirror did not fog up. Doctor Lyolya placed her stethoscope against my chest to determine if my heart was still beating. She did not hear a beat and concluded that I had died. Doctor Lyolya and the nurse then lifted my body onto the stretcher and carried me out of the room. I was aware that they were moving me, but I had neither the strength nor the will to speak. I lost consciousness.

I was told later that Doctor Lyolya decided to bring my body into her office rather then upstairs where the children's corpses were kept. She hoped that I might still be alive. She brought a kerosene lamp into the office and lighted it in order to warm the air in the small room. Then she injected me with a dose of glucose and left to take care of the other children. When she returned I had regained consciousness; I had returned from the dead. Doctor Lyolya was so amazed and happy that she would check on me again and again with her stethoscope in order to listen to my heart beat.

I discovered in the days that followed that Doctor Lyolya had been one of mother's students. She said that she liked mother's lessons in physiology so much that she chose to become a physician. I told Doctor Lyolya that mother had experienced an accident and that she was in the hospital on Line Fifteen. Doctor Lyolya was happy to hear that mother was alive, and thereafter she visited mother and informed her that I was still alive and that I would soon be better.

Doctor Lyolya disappeared one evening, and we would not see her again. After leaving the children's house she walked to her home. Her apartment was located in a district of the city that was shelled that evening. It is possible that a fascist shell killed her. If she was injured she might have been brought to a hospital and then later evacuated from Leningrad.

Doctor Lyolya's influence upon me is evident even now. She had an unusual habit whenever she was in a stressful situation; she would draw treble clefs on a notepad and that would help calm her. If there was an air raid she would take out a sheet of paper and begin to draw images of treble clefs. It was a habit that I adopted. Whenever I find myself in a stressful situation I begin drawing the treble clef, and it too helps calm me. I also remember Doctor Lyolya as the lady who saved my life.

Chapter Eighteen

Olga Symanovskaya

FEBRUARY 1942

Before the war Olga was a teacher of mathematics in the school where mother taught. She didn't look like a typical teacher. She always wore bright colored dresses. Her hair was cut short, and she combed it like most young men wore their hair. She was always happy and loud. Olga was not married. The other teachers felt that she was quite eccentric.

The students liked Olga and asked her to join them whenever they played soccer. She would join them, and she kicked the ball as well and as hard as the boys. Before she went out into the playing field she would take off the white beret that she always wore. She handed it to one of the students watching the game from the sidelines, and the student would hold the beret until the game came to an end.

Maybe Olga's love for children brought her to our children's house. There was so many of us. Most of us were from eight to ten years old. We were all so very weak. All day every day we would lie quietly in our beds. We would move and sit up only when it was time to eat.

Olga entered our large room toward the beginning of February 1942. She was wearing her bright white beret. She walked to the windows, pulled to the sides the black-out curtains and flooded the room with light. Then she said with a commanding voice: "Come let's all sit up and do our morning exercises." We just looked at her and thought that she was mad. If she wanted to do some morning exercises we were going to let her do them alone. We would watch. But the exercises that Olga wanted us to do were more mental than

physical. She wanted us to repeat out loud a two-line stanza that she had written. I still remember the words:

> We have survived the mouth of January; and we will survive the mouth of Feb-
> ruary; when the mouth of March arrives, we will sing songs of happiness and
> joy!

Olga repeated the stanzas over and over and we just watched her and listened
silently.

Our attitude did not discourage Olga. The next day she was back. "Dear
children," she said, "come on let's do our morning exercises." She must have
noticed that several children in the room had died during the night because
their beds were empty. Yet she wanted us, the living, to have a positive out-
look, and she tried to instill that within us. Olga came every morning, and she
would stay with us until into the evening. She talked to us, and she prevented
us from nodding off or thinking about hunger and death. Gradually she
brought us out of our listless state of existence, and each morning we tried to
repeat after her:

> We have survived the month of January, and we will survive the month of Feb-
> ruary; when the month of March arrives, we will sing songs of happiness and
> joy!

We began to look forward to Olga's arrival in the mornings, and we hated to
see her leave in the evenings. We felt that the cheerfulness that Olga brought
into our room evaporated with her departure.

One day we were told that Olga had fallen while she was walking home
from the children's house. The fall must have hurt her quite seriously because
she was unable to stand up and would no longer be visiting us. We received
this information from one of the older students who attended the school
where Olga and mother taught. Olga must have told the student to visit us,
and in honor of Olga we recited together the stanzas that Olga had taught us:

> We have survived the month of January, and we will survive the month of Feb-
> ruary; when the month of March arrives, we will sing songs of happiness and
> joy!

At the end of March we were still doing our morning exercises. I believe
that the recitation of Olga's stanzas helped strengthen those of us who did survive the months of February and March. Each new child in our room would
join us in our morning exercises. The new children were assigned to the beds
that were left empty by those who had died. In April we would recite together:

We have survived the month of March, and we will survive the month of April; when the month of May arrives, we will sing songs of happiness and joy.

Each year on January 27 many of the people who survived the siege of Leningrad come together and celebrate. On January 27, 1944, the blockade of the city came to an end. Those of us who knew Olga as a teacher or as an encourager always set aside a few minutes during our celebration to express our respect for and gratitude toward Olga. Together we recite the stanzas that she taught us in the children's house as a morning exercise.

Chapter Nineteen

Olya and Seryozha, Milochka and Polinochka

EARLY SPRING 1942

In the spring there were two children in each bed at the children's house. The black-out curtains covered the windows, and it was so cold in our room that the children in each bed would lie close to each other to stay warm. Most of us were starving, most of us did not experience the sensation of pain, and most of us no longer believed that we would survive the blockade. We believed that our country would be victorious, but we did not believe that we would be alive to celebrate Victory Day. We were sure that there would be a time when the children in the Soviet Union would again play in the sunshine under a blue clear sky and celebrate the New Year around a New Year tree; however, this would be done without us. We would die, we believed, before then.

Death chose the weakest of us. Death had been standing next to the bed of Olya, but it was unable to take her because her brother Seryozha was still alive. The two shared the same bed. Olya was twelve years old and Seryozha was five. He was small in stature, thin and blond. He slept almost all the time and would sit up only when a spoon of food touched his lips. He never opened his eyes. He would eat his portion of food and after that he would eat Olya's portion; then he would lie down and fall asleep. The doctor and nurse tried to persuade Olya to eat, but she refused to eat. She wanted to give her portion to her brother, and each day Olya became thinner and appeared weaker. In spite of the extra portions of food that were given to Seryozha, he died. Olya kissed his cold face and would not permit the doctor or nurse to take him away from her for quite some time.

When they finally did remove Seryozha's body, Olya just sighed and died. She no longer wanted to live and permitted death to take her as well.

Milochka and Polinochka were placed in the bed that had been shared by Olya and Seryozha. They were sisters who arrived in the children's house in the spring. They looked well fed as if they had come to us from pre-war times. They not only walked but they had the physical strength to run and jump and play hide and seek. They had pretty dresses and wore expensive shoes. I would often watch them play, and sometimes I wondered if I was asleep and that the sisters were two characters in a dream.

Military officers would often visit Milochka and Polinochka. They would bring them food like out of a fairy tale. The sisters were given large sticks of chocolate packaged in special wrapping that was decorated with pictures of ship anchors. Cans of milk sweetened with sugar and cans of meat were also given to the sisters. The girls drank and ate the gifts of food as they laughed and talked to each other. They did not share their gifts with the rest of us. They seemed to be oblivious of us; it was as if we did not exist. Sometimes they would sing a Ukrainian song, but I was so weak that I could never stay awake long enough to hear them complete the song.

One day the district in which the children's house was located was shelled by fascists. The shelling began suddenly and the shells did not whistle to warn us of their coming; they just exploded. Milochka and Polinochka were so frightened by the explosions that they crawled under their bed and began screaming in Ukrainian: "Oh Trouble! Oh Disaster!" It was apparent that they had never been exposed to artillery shelling. After the shelling stopped, it took the teachers working at the children's house quite some time to persuade the sisters to come out from under their bed. I noticed that the teachers were much more gentle with Milochka and Polinochka than they were with the rest of us in the room.

Milochka and Polinochka did not survive the war. During a second shelling of our district, the sisters died. They were not struck by a shell, and their bodies were not touched physically. I believe they died from fright. The sisters appeared healthy physically but were weak mentally, and thus fear and terror killed them.

Sometimes when I feel pain, emotional or physical pain, I remember Olya. She was weak physically and starving. Yet she kept herself alive until her brother's death. She was strong mentally. The caring attitude she demonstrated toward her brother was heroic, and she would die with dignity.

Chapter Twenty

Little Alexander (Alik)

SUMMER 1942

Alik was no more than four years old. His mother had died, and a military officer brought him wrapped in a blanket to our children's house. The officer said the boy's name was Alik. Nobody knew for sure if his name was Alexander or Alexey. Alik was so weak that he slept most of the time. When he was awake he remained quiet. When he was asked a question he looked at the person asking the question but did not answer. We thought that Alik had lost the ability to speak. We had been told that there were children who were so traumatized by the horrors of the war that they were unable to speak. Alik would eat his portion of soup quickly, ask with inquiring eyes if he could have some more and then lay down to fall asleep.

During the summer season our life improved. We went outside in the courtyard behind the children's house and walked for short periods of time in the sun. The warmth of the sunlight felt so good. We could feel ourselves grow stronger especially after each of us was fed a half of an egg a day. The eggs had been airlifted into Leningrad and were excellent. The smell of the eggs reminded me of peace and life before the war.

After Alik finished eating his first half egg he suddenly began to speak. I don't remember what he said but the words that he used expressed his joy, and every one who heard him smiled. He had difficulty mouthing the words, but the more he practiced the more fluent he became. Thereafter, he would talk from morning till evening. As he talked he would smile. He was the youngest child in the room, and the girls liked to take care of him. Alik enjoyed the attention that the girls gave him, and he even permitted them to help him remove his trousers that were held up with suspenders.

Alik and I were together in the room during an artillery attack. The explosions began suddenly and were so loud that many of the children and the adults in the children's house rushed to the back staircase of the building and down the stairs. I remained in the room because I did not feel strong enough to run with the others. Alik remained as well. He had crept under his bed and was crying out loud. While Alik was still under the bed a huge explosion shook the entire building. I could feel the floor move, and I could hear glass windows breaking and the air around me became filled with dust. Alik screamed, and then the room became silent. I was afraid that Alik was hurt or even killed so I got out of my bed slowly and reached under his bed. He grabbed my hand, crawled out from under the bed, threw his arms around me and begged me to carry him to a place that was safe.

Together we left the room and headed for the staircase. At the staircase we could hear the voices of the other children who were already downstairs. Their voices were drowned out by a deafening explosion. A shell had hit the building next to the children's house. We could hear the glass of windows shatter, doors break and the building next to ours fall. The air became red with brick dust. It seemed as if my eyes were covered with blood.

The force of the explosion had pushed me against a wall by the staircase, and I felt a strong jabbing pain in my back. Everything happened so quickly that I had to re-gather my thoughts. I remembered that Alik had been with me by the staircase, and I needed to find him. I discovered that he was right in front of me. The force of the explosion had pushed me against Alik who was sandwiched between me and the wall. His body was trembling, but he was not hurt.

No one was injured by the explosion except me. I would continue to feel a jabbing pain in my back, and later when the doctor examined me it was decided that I should lie motionless on a solid flat surface which I did. Gradually the pain subsided. During the days of recovery, Alik would spend many hours by my bedside. Often after I awakened from a nap and opened my eyes I would see Alik standing by my bed looking at me.

The shelling to which we were exposed in the summer of 1942 would have a devastating effect on Alik's young mind. The little boy began to stutter. When he wanted something to eat he would say "Ah-give ah-Alik ah-a piece of ah-bread." After a while, he would repeat his sentence over and over without understanding its meaning. It seemed as if he was astonished by his ability to speak. As time went on he stopped repeating the request and only made the sound "ah."

After the blockade ended Alik's father found his son at the children's house and took him home. Alik's name the father told us was Alexander. The name Alexander meant nothing to Alik. In fact, he did not recognize his father. As

Alik was about to leave with his father he began to cry, and suddenly he uttered "Ah-give ah-Alik ah-a piece of ah-bread."

The explosion that threw Alik and me against the wall in the children's house made me a heroine. Someone decided that I had saved Alik's life by shielding his body from the blast of the explosion. The fact that Alik wanted to be with me at all times thereafter was proof for many at the children's house that I had saved Alik's life. I tried to explain that the force of the explosion had pushed my body against Alik, but the adults in the children's house just smiled at my explanation. They believed I was being modest, and they appreciated it. Later someone informed my mother about the heroic act of her daughter. I tried to explain to her that I had nothing to do with saving Alik's life. To my astonishment she did not believe me. She believed that her daughter was a heroine, and no one not even her daughter was going to convince her that it was not so.

To this day I feel pain in my back. It is something that I have learned to live with since my incident with Alik. On days when the pain is especially intense I think of the little boy whose body was shielded by mine during the explosion. His mind, however, was unprotected and thus was traumatized by the experience; I hope not forever.

Chapter Twenty-One

Summer in the Children's House

SUMMER 1942
THE BOY ALEXANDER "SASHA"

Sasha was brought to the children's house in order to recover from the sur-
geries that were performed on him at a hospital. He was eleven or twelve
years old. His mother and brother had starved to death. Sasha had wrapped
their bodies in bed sheets and had pulled them on a sled, one at a time, to a
location in the city where corpses were to be brought. Starvation had taken
from Sasha the two most important people in his life, and bringing their bodies to Leningrad's makeshift cemetery magnified the reality of his loss. After
he returned home, his apartment building was struck by several artillery
shells. One of the shells tore off the lower half of his left arm and badly dam-
aged the lower part of his leg. At the hospital the doctors amputated his left
arm up to the elbow and the leg up to the knee.

Sasha was thin, he looked pale and he was quiet. At night in the children's
house I would see him cry but not out loud. Everyday Doctor Lyolya carefully changed the bandages on his arm and leg. If a part of a bandage took
with it some of the hardened crusted blood, Sasha would grimace but would
not cry out.

One day Sasha said out loud that he did not want to live anymore. He then
turned his face to the wall and remained silent. The next morning Sasha's bed
was empty. Next to the bed were his crutches. Everyone in the room knew
that Sasha had died, and his death shocked all of us. Each of us was barely
alive but we had our arms and legs, and we lived with the hope that one day
our arms and legs would be strong again. Sasha did not have this hope. He
died because he had lost the will to live.

After Sasha's death we realized that in order to live we had to become active and involved with each other. The silence of the room was broken with the sound of our weak voices. We began talking to each other. Someone would ask about the development along the military front. Someone else would ask how much longer the war would last. Others raised their bodies in seated positions in their beds. We then asked our doctor to pull away from the windows the black-out curtains. It was snowing outside, but the sun was visible beyond the winter clouds, and its rays, though dimmed, illuminated the room. For us the light represented life, and as it entered the room it chased away the darkness of death.

I was so moved by Sasha's death that I expressed my thoughts in a poem. As I whispered the words tears came to my eyes. Lena, whose bed was next to mine, heard me whisper the poem. She took out a small piece of paper and asked me to repeat it. When I finished reciting it she read it back to me:

> In our children's house
> Sasha used to often weep.
> He had just one leg,
> And had lost the lower
> Half of his arm.
> He had buried his family
> And was alone.
> That is the reason Sasha
> Wept
>
> In our children's house.
> Now only the crutches
> Stand
> Gathering dust near his bed
> Could he not walk
> And yesterday he said
> That he did not want to live
> He became silent forever.
>
> Sasha, Sasha, please live.
> I have two arms,
> I have two legs,
> I will help you
> I can and I will.
>
> In our children's house
> Sasha would often weep.
> Now, his two friends
> Lena and I weep for him.
> In our children's house

Sasha has died.
Now only his crutches stand
Gathering dust near his bed.

Again a "Messerschmitt"
Flies over the children's house.
For the remainder of my life
⌈I will hate fascism,   ⌉
│I will hate war,   │
⌊And I will desire peace.   ⌋

Lena read the poem again so that all the children could hear it. Many of them wept in response, but the response was significant. When tears come to a person's eyes, it means that his or her soul is still alive.

When Doctor Lyolya entered the room Lena read the poem to her. Doctor Lyolya was so impressed with the poem that she asked permission to rewrite it and send it to the newspaper for publication. She rewrote the poem in a small notebook, tore out the page upon which she had written it and placed the notebook in my hands. She said the rest of the pages in the notebook were blank and that I should fill them with poems. I whispered to her that I did not want to write any more poems because the thoughts and emotions that I conveyed in my poems were frightening. Doctor Lyolya wanted me to keep the notebook, and after she left the room Lena and I examined it for a long time. It was a pre-war notebook and its pages were made with good quality paper. I would keep the notebook throughout the remainder of the war, and at the end of the war it was still empty.

DENNIS DAVIDOV

Dennis was brought to the children's house in the summer of 1942. He was a teenager with thick lips and long legs. Maybe this is why he was so clumsy. He was different from the other children in that he was shy and reserved. Dennis was polite and intelligent but could not answer with assertiveness. He would not complain to our teachers. He hated confrontation and the use of force. He would often cover his face with his hands and say: "Please don't hurt me. Forgive me if I did something wrong."

There were boys at the house who would offend Dennis, and the worst of the trouble makers was Leonid Smirnov. He was nine years old, but his wrinkled face gave him the appearance of an old man. He had a hostile disposition, and he would quarrel and argue with everyone in our room. Nobody liked him not even the teachers. One teacher told us that the cold of the past winter season had entered Leonid and that with each of his acts of hostility it was coming out of his body. The teacher's explanation was quite believable. However, we did not understand why the cold of the winter had taken residence in Leonid alone. We too had experienced the fierce winter of 1941–1942, and we could not imagine that Leonid had suffered any more than the rest of us.

Leonid liked to offend Dennis by saying hurtful things about Dennis, by laughing at him and by shoving and pushing him. Why did Leonid do this? Maybe it was because Dennis looked so different from the others. Dennis had ears that came forward and stuck straight out and Leonid and his companions made fun of them. They laughed at his trousers which were too large around the waist. Someone had stolen Dennis' belt, and in order to prevent the trousers from falling to the floor Dennis had to hold them up with one of his hands. When a boy would pinch Dennis or kick him, he would lose his grip and his trousers would fall to the floor exposing his long legs that were so thin that they looked like toothpicks. When this happened all the boys would laugh. It was a pitiful sight. Most of the girls in the room including myself sympathized with Dennis and tried to defend him from Leonid and his bullies.

One of our teachers tried to help Dennis. She told the children that our Dennis was a descendant of Dennis Davidov, a hero during Russia's war against Napoleon in 1812. The information conveyed by our teacher was an attempt to gain for Dennis the boys' respect, but the attempt had a negative effect. The boys wondered how Dennis Davidov, a brilliant military hero, could have such a pathetic descendant as our Dennis.

Then a sudden change occurred in the demeanor of Dennis. He acquired a belt and no longer had to hold on to his trousers. The acquisition of the belt was an important event in the children's house, and it was discussed by many of the children. The belt was old, but it was a genuine leather belt. We who had felt sorry for Dennis were now so happy for him. Leonid on the other hand had stopped abusing Dennis not because he had a change of heart but because Dennis no longer appeared to be a weakling.

Where did Dennis get the belt? Who could have presented this gift to Dennis? In time, we learned that Dennis had not eaten his daily portion of sugar cubes for many days, and when he had saved up enough cubes he exchanged the sugar for the old belt. The children in the house considered the actions of Dennis heroic. He had been willing to risk his life to purchase the belt. His actions reaffirmed to the children that Dennis was truly a deserved descendant of Dennis Davidov.

Dennis became such a hero that the children invited him to join what was considered the fraternity of the house. He accepted our invitation with a shy but thankful smile. He would never allow anyone to abuse him again, and nobody ever tried.

DIMA LYAKHOVICH

Dima was brought to the children's house in May. He was eleven years old. He had dark eyes, black hair and a large mouth. There was a graceful manner about him, and he made an effort to be polite.

Dima suffered from dystrophy and chronic diarrhea. Whenever he would have an accident caused by his diarrhea one of the teachers would have to wash him and change the sheets on his bed. The accidents were embarrassing for Dima, and he tried to apologize to the teacher who had to wash him and change the sheets. He found it difficult to apologize because he was so refined in the way he acted and spoke. He could not come up with a proper word for his accident.

The teacher treated Dima with kindness and told him not to hesitate to call her if he should have another accident. She said that some time in the future Dima would be cured of dystrophy and diarrhea. Dima was so grateful for the teacher's attitude and comments that he took her hand and kissed it. The teacher gave assistance to the other children in various ways, but nobody would kiss her hands. The teacher told Dima that she did not want him to kiss her hand again, but he would not obey. He would kiss her hand each time that she attended his needs. He said that his father had done this with his mother while she cared for his father when he was ill.

Dima died during the night. The dystrophy and the chronic diarrhea had killed him. When the teacher found Dima dead in the morning she stood motionless next to his bed for a long time. Then she took his body and washed it. She wrapped the body carefully in a clean blanket and carried it out of the room.

She would not return until the next day. She looked sad and tired. We thought she would say something about Dima, but she didn't. We knew that Dima's death had affected her emotionally and we believed it would be cruel to ask her about the person who had become so important in her life.

Later the teacher told me that she had buried Dima in the city's cemetery. She said that she wanted Dima's body to be buried immediately. She did not want to wait for the team of soldiers, assigned to bury corpses, to bury Dima. That could take days. She told me that she had paid someone to bury Dima and she gave the person several pieces of bread. The teacher sighed and whispered that she had planned to adopt Dima after the war, but fate had made that impossible. She added that if I should ever choose to marry someone like

Dima, then no one would ever have to be concerned about my wellbeing. It was an interesting statement, but I was a young girl and I would not comprehend what she meant until much later.

BISMARCK AND ARISTOTLE

Bismarck and Aristotle were brought into our room in May. They were orphans. Their mothers had died recently, and both boys were suffering from the loss of their parents. Bismarck was the boy's last name; we didn't know his first name. Aristotle was the other boy's first name; he didn't tell us his last name. Because they arrived at the same time, we identified them as a pair and called them Bismarck and Aristotle. We discovered that their names were appropriate when somebody told us about Otto von Bismarck, the former Chancellor of Prussia, and Aristotle, the philosopher of ancient Greece. Our Bismarck was unfriendly and usually had a frown on his face and we imagined that the Prussian Chancellor, who did such terrible things, had a similar disposition. Our Aristotle had a large forehead and we believed that the philosopher of ancient Greece, with all of that knowledge stored up in his brain, probably had a large head. That is why we would sometimes call the boys "Chancellor and Philosopher."

Bismarck and Aristotle were among those in the children's house who were being prepared for an evacuation from the city. It meant that each day they had to practice walking. They would get out of their beds and walk from bed to bed throughout the room. They would support themselves by grabbing hold of the legs of the beds. If one of them felt strong enough he would go to the long corridor outside of our room and try to walk down the corridor and back without any support. If a child was able to walk up and down the corridor several times he or she was declared ready for the evacuation. Bismarck and Aristotle had passed the test, and they were declared strong enough to be taken out of the city.

The children who were to be evacuated had to prepare themselves mentally for their upcoming trip. Everyone knew that the trip across Lake Ladoga was dangerous. German aircraft flew over the lake and dropped their bombs on the vehicles that brought the citizens of Leningrad across the lake and beyond the blockade. We had been told that only half of the children who were transported along the Road of Life reached the opposite shore of the lake. The others never made it. We were told that during the summer after the ice over Lake Ladoga had melted, boats were used to bring the children across the lake. The Germans would bomb the boats and after a boat was hit and sunk the white Panamas that the children had worn rose to the surface of the water. They were like water lilies that had been dropped in the water as funeral flowers. That is why many children in our children's house had difficulty sleeping during the week before their evacuation. At night they would get out of bed and stare out of the windows into "white night" sky as they pondered the dangers of their future trip.

One night a heart-rending cry came from the corridor. As we entered the hallway we saw Aristotle lying on the floor with blood slowly coming out of his mouth. The locked door to the pantry in which food was stored had been jammed open, and some food had been taken out. Apparently, Aristotle had entered the corridor, for who knows what reason, and saw someone steal the food. The thief then murdered Aristotle who was a witness to the crime.

Who in the children's house would both steal and murder? Most of the children suspected it was Bismarck. He was unfriendly, and all the children decided that he was the most likely to commit such a terrible act. Having decided that Bismarck was the murderer, several of the older boys in the children's house cornered Bismarck and beat him. Thereafter, he was removed from our house and everyone suspected that he had been taken to prison. The authorities probably moved him to another children's house because they were afraid that he would be murdered by the older boys if he remained with us. I would not see Bismarck again.

Shortly after Bismarck's departure I heard a doctor and a nurse who were on duty discuss the murder of Aristotle. The one whispered to the other that the person who murdered Aristotle had to be strong physically, and that eliminated Bismarck as a suspect. He was not strong enough to have done it. If that was true, it was possible that the thief and murderer was still in our midst. Maybe the murderer was a stranger who had entered the house in search of food. It was a frightening and unsettling thought, and it caused me to tremble.

MARGARET (RITOCHKA) LOSEVA

Of all the girls in the children's house Ritochka had the most dynamic personality. She was suffering from dystrophy and scurvy when she was brought into our room, but she was optimistic and seemed to be full of energy. She was independent and loved her freedom, yet she was so approachable. With her friendly smile she seemed to invite conversation.

Ritochka was also the most attractive of all the girls. She had a halo of golden hair around her head. The light locks that hung down at the sides had natural curls and formed little ringlets around her temples. The rest of the hair was arranged in plaits. It was cut just above the shoulders, and the plaited hair bounced up and down with each movement of Ritochka's head.

Ritochka and Tamara Gladieva were the poets in our room. Ritochka was an optimist, and her poetry reflected her optimism. She was sure that she would survive the war and that her mother would return from the military front to take her home. She was certain that her grandmother would regain her strength and that the old lady would re-experience the life that she had known before the war. Ritochka's poetry gave us hope and made us smile. Tamara, however, was sad and her poems would bring tears to our eyes. She would describe the loneliness and the feeling of abandonment in our children's house. "Don't forget us," she would write, "the children who have lost their mothers." Poetry is an expression of feelings, and we loved to listen to Ritochka and Tamara as they recited their poems.

IRMAH LIVSHITZ

There was no child who was more sad than Irmah. She became an orphan when she was only nine years old. Her mother and brother died from starvation, and her father became insane. The deaths of her mother and brother and the loss of her father so grieved Irmah, that her face was the face of sorrow. Although she never wept, her eyes were filled with tears. Such an unhappy person would not live long.

It was Ritochka who brought Irmah back to life. The two became close friends and spent most of their time together each day. After a while they invited me to join them in their activities. It was through our times together that I re-experienced the happiness of friendship. I also began to feel happy that I was alive.

Irmah survived the war, and I would meet her many years later. We talked about the war and the experiences that we shared in the children's house. I reminisced about the time she had brought me her portion of sugar after I was brought to the isolation ward. I had become ill, and the doctor did not want the other children to be exposed to my illness. I was told by the teacher who looked after me that Irmah made sure each day that I drank the cup of hot water in which she had stirred her portion of sugar. As I talked about this incident Irmah had a puzzled look on her face. She did not remember visiting me in the isolation ward. "Do you remember," she asked, "giving me your bread when, for some reason, I was not given my portion?" I did not remember. The incidents we recalled reminded me how natural it had been for friends to assist each other during the war.

ALEXANDER (SASHA) BAYKEYEV

Sasha arrived at the children's house on crutches. He had lost one of his legs. He never told us how he lost it, and we never asked him to tell us because we knew that he did not want to talk about it. Somebody said that he lost it trying to save a child from a building that was being shelled. The building collapsed while he was inside, and his leg was crushed so badly that it had to be amputated. Others said that Sasha had lost it while fighting the fascists along one of the military fronts. Nobody knew for sure. We did know that he was about thirteen or fourteen years old, and we considered him a hero.

Sasha was a giving person who tried to be of service to others. He would comfort the children who were in pain. He himself was in pain, but he never wept or complained. He would tell stories or fairy tales to cheer up the children who were sad. He would smile at the children who became upset and let them know in his own way that everything was going to be fine. Sometimes he would give a portion of his food to a child who was particularly weak. Sasha became the heart and soul of our little community; he became more important to us than the adults who took care of us. We admired and loved Sasha. Whatever Sasha said we accepted as truth. If Sasha asked us to do something we would do it because we wanted to please him.

Sasha always wore the red neck tie that was given to a Young Pioneer. He wore it around his neck and with pride. He was the only one to do so in our children's house. Apparently no one else had remembered to take theirs with them to the children's house. Sasha, however, had remembered to take his tie, and for him it was a badge of honor.

Sasha was placed with the group of children who were to be evacuated from Leningrad. He was stronger physically then most of the children in our house. He could move around easily with his crutches. He would often joke that his crutches were too big and that their size permitted him to make long strides as he walked. When Sasha moved up and down the length of the corridor he did so with little difficulty; he was faster than all the others who were in the group to be evacuated.

Sasha was unable to sleep on the night before his evacuation. I watched him sitting by a window staring at the outside world. What thoughts were running through his mind? Was he thinking about the trip across Lake Ladoga? It was such a dangerous trip. Was he afraid that a fascist shell would send him to the bottom of the lake?

The next morning Sasha and several other children boarded a truck that had arrived for their evacuation. Sasha was lifted up into the bed of the truck and sat next to the other children who were to be evacuated. The rest of us watched from windows and waved. Quietly, we wished our departing friends a safe journey.

Sasha was not evacuated. He returned on his crutches to the children's house late in the evening of the day that the truck arrived for his evacuation. He told the authorities that he wanted to stay in Leningrad. He said that he wanted to contribute to its defense in some way, and he believed he could best do this by staying.

Two days later Sasha would leave the children's house to make his contribution toward victory. We don't know where he went. At that time many young people who were Sasha's age worked in factories in which military supplies were being made. These young people worked as volunteers, and they were fed and housed in the factories. It would have been characteristic for Sasha to volunteer his services. He was such a giving person; he was always thinking about the welfare of others.

THE WATER IN PALMS

Going to the bathhouse was a grand occasion for all of us. The bathhouse was located on the Eighth Line of the city, and this meant that we had to walk a long distance. It must have been quite an interesting scene to see a long line of children walk down the sidewalk. Our legs and arms were thin, our knees and elbows seemed so large and our heads were bald. The reason for the bath was to rid our bodies of lice.

When we arrived at the bathhouse we washed ourselves with purpose. No one talked. Our supply of water was limited, and each of us used every drop of warm water that had been allotted to us. As we bathed the teachers urged us to hurry. They wanted to get us back to the children's house before the shelling began.

As I stepped out of the bathhouse I slipped and fell on the dirty floor in front of the bathhouse door. It was a disgusting accident. I had just washed myself, it was something that I had longed to do for six months and now I was dirty again. I turned to one of the teachers and begged her to permit me to go back into the bathhouse to wash off the dirt. She hesitated but finally consented and followed me back into the bathhouse.

When we entered the bathing room of the bathhouse another group of girls from the children's house had already entered to wash themselves. The teacher explained to the girls that I had fallen in the dirt. She asked them if they would be willing to share their water with me. One of the girls cupped her hands together and scooped up some water from her basin and poured the water over my dirty shoulder. The others in the group followed the first girl's example until their handfuls of water had washed the dirt from my body. I was so happy that I started to laugh. The girls laughed with me, and one of the smaller girls started to slap the water in her basin creating a spray of water that shot up like a water fountain. It reminded me of fireworks that are shot off during a celebration. I returned to the children's house clean and with deep appreciation for the kindness that the girls had demonstrated to me.

MY FIRST PRAYER
JUNE 1942

One of the teachers at the children's house was Barbara Alexandrovna. She was kind and had beautiful hair that had turned gray. She had a wonderful smile, but she rarely smiled. She had received word that her son Gorgy who was in the military had disappeared, and she worried about his welfare. Barbara never wept in our presence, but we could see traces of tears in her kind eyes. We tried to comfort her by telling her about soldiers who had been declared lost but who later returned home safely. Barbara would listen and smile that wonderful smile as tears filled her eyes.

One night I was awakened by a prayer that Barbara whispered to God. There were days when she would not go home since there was no one there waiting for her. She would sleep in our room and at the same time be there for us throughout the night. On the night that her prayer awakened me I got out of bed and saw Barbara on her knees with her elbows resting on the windowsill of one of the windows. Her eyes were open, and she was looking out into the white night of Leningrad. I could see her lips move as she was whispering a prayer to God.

After Barbara finished her prayer she got up and saw me standing nearby watching her. She whispered to me that she had prayed to God to protect her son from war and to return him to her. She did not want anyone to know that she had been praying and asked me not to tell the others that I had seen her pray. I promised that I would not tell anyone.

After seeing Barbara pray I began to pray as well. I had never been taught to pray, and I did not know how to go about it. I decided to just talk to God. I started by saying, "Dear and dearest God! Please, do what is necessary to bring the war to an end quickly and bring Barbara's son Gorgy home." The name Gorgy is an unusual name so I emphasized in my prayer that the son's name was Gorgy not Georgy. I was afraid that God was not familiar with the name Gorgy. I also asked God to protect my mother Pavla Dmitriyevna. I

repeated mother's name as well. Pavla is also an unusual name, and I suspected that God had never heard it.

   Gorgy never returned home. His disappearance remains a mystery. Barbara
decided that her son was probably killed in battle and that he died before she
began praying for his protection. She believed that if she had started praying
for him earlier God would have protected him and brought him home.

Chapter Twenty-Two

The Evacuation

JULY 1942

In the summer of 1942 I was able to walk the length of the long corridor in the children's house and was declared strong enough to be evacuated. My evacuation took place in July. I along with many other children was placed on a truck that was one of several within a convoy of trucks headed for the south-eastern shoreline of Lake Ladoga. At the western shoreline the convoy was bombed by the Germans and many of the children within our group were killed. Many children were also wounded and were carried to safety by the women who had been assigned as guardians of the children.

Mother had been assigned to be one of our guardians. From a distance I could see her carrying a wounded child in her arms. His name was Marick Altshooler. Several other children, frightened by terrible explosions and the human destruction that the bombs had caused, clutched to mother's skirt as she tried to carry Marick to safety. I would not see mother again until after we arrived along the opposite shoreline of Ladoga Lake. We were brought across the lake in boats. I was so happy to see mother that I stayed close by her side so that we would not be separated from each other again.

On the eastern side of the lake a train was waiting to take us further east. Just as everyone boarded the train German airplanes appeared and the fascists began dropping their deadly bombs with the intention of destroying the train. The German airmen knew that the train was not being used for military pur-poses because a large Red Cross had been painted on the sides of each car. Fortunately, the train was not hit during the air raid, and as the train picked up speed the Germans were left behind. Our destination was the Yaroslavl City region where we boarded another train.

We finally reached a village named Gorelovo. At the village the authorities gave my mother a teaching position at a large children's house that would become the home for many children who were evacuated from Leningrad. There was no physician on duty at the children's house so mother, having earned a degree in biology, provided the children with much needed medical care. Most of the children were orphans, and many showed symptoms of dystrophy. Through the care of mother and other teachers at the children's house, the children recovered and regained their strength. Only one of the 120 children who were brought to the children's house died.

On May 9, 1945, the woman in charge of the village post office received the announcement that the war was over. At that time, mother and I were living in one of the rooms of the post office. The post officer was so excited with the news that she knocked on our bedroom wall to awaken us and tell us the good news. We were so happy that we jumped up and down and shouted: "The war is over!" "The war is over!" "The war is over!"

Mother and I returned to Leningrad after Victory Day. When we arrived, we discovered that our apartment was being occupied by strangers. These people were very kind and promised to vacate our apartment as soon as they were able to find another place of residence. They left several days later, but in the meantime mother and I lived with Elena Tissler who was a neighbor. She was the only other person in our large apartment building who had survived the war.

In Leningrad mother continued her career as a teacher, and I continued my studies. After graduating from school, I was accepted as a student at Leningrad State University. There my major area of study was biology. After earning my degree at the university, I moved to Moscow hoping to earn my doctor's degree. After I defended my doctoral dissertation, I began my career working with and doing research on the pathophysiology of the nervous and immune systems of human beings. Moscow is where I made my permanent residence; however, I often feel beautiful Leningrad, the place of my birth, tugging at my heart. To this day I find it difficult to consider myself a citizen of Moscow.

Chapter Twenty-Three

Other Survivors

In recent years Svetlana has attended the annual celebration commemorating the end of the blockade around Leningrad. The celebration is held on January 27 in St. Petersburg (Leningrad was renamed St. Petersburg in 1991), and it is attended by hundreds of Russians who survived the blockade. Svetlana has made the acquaintance of some of these survivors and they have shared with her their memories of life behind the blockade. They talked about the experiences they had in common such as the shelling and bombing of Leningrad by the Germans, the cold and freezing temperatures during the winter months of 1941–1942 and the shortage of food and other necessities. They also discovered that each had been exposed to events and incidents that were unique to them. The brief but poignant accounts of Peter Tzvetkov, Lidochka Karasyova, Vera Gryaznova, Galya Iplisova, Allochka Ivanova and Ireenka are recorded in this, the last, chapter of the book.

PETER TZVETKOV
1941–1942

Peter said that his knowledge of war began when he was told that Germany had invaded the Soviet Union. He was just five years old when it happened. He remembered that his father left home to fight against the fascists. He also recalled his mother crying when his father said goodbye. Peter learned quickly that war inflicts pain and suffering on human beings of all ages.

From the very beginning of the blockade the Germans bombed the city district where Peter and his mother lived. They rented an apartment on Tauride

Drive, near the main water treatment plant of Leningrad. The German bombers tried often to destroy the water plant and thus deprive the citizens of their drinking water. During the air raids Peter and his mother would hurry to the basement of their apartment complex to seek shelter. The explosions of the German bombs were so powerful that the apartment building would literally jump with each bomb that was dropped. Soon three of the five large buildings on Tauride Drive lay in ruins.

In October the city's main water line was struck by a bomb. A fountain of water shot up from a gaping hole in the ground, and thereafter many people in the city did not receive drinking water. From that time forward Peter and his mother along with thousands of other Leningraders had to make their way to one of the city's rivers each day to get their supply of water. The winter season had already begun, and the rivers were covered with ice. The water that spilled out of the buckets that were used by the people also turned to ice. Thus the banks of the rivers became coated with ice. The ice made it difficult for many people and impossible for some people to make their way down the riverbanks to get the needed water. Climbing back up the riverbanks was even more difficult. Many people who were weak from starvation were unable to make the climb. They would fall on the ice, and if someone did not give them assistance they would eventually die where they had fallen.

During the winter of 1941 there were only two families that inhabited the large apartment building where Peter and his mother lived. At night people who lived in other neighborhoods would break into the building to get firewood. They would take pieces of furniture that the former residents had left. They would also break into small manageable pieces the wooden doors of the apartments, and they would tear up the wooden floors. These people were not criminals; they simply wanted to stay warm and alive, and the wood that they gathered from the vacated apartments helped them do that.

Peter and his mother left their home and moved to the apartment used by Peter's two aunts. The room that Peter and his mother shared was small and cold. Peter's mother worked at a military hospital, and while she was at the hospital Peter was under the care of his aunts. Peter was constantly hungry, and once he almost fainted from hunger. Seeing Peter lie motionless and assuming that he had fallen asleep, one aunt said to his other aunt, "He is asleep. Now let's have some tea." When Peter heard his aunt's remark, he sat up believing that he would be given some food. He was given only hot water.

One morning Peter's aunts were unable to leave the apartment and acquire their daily rations of bread from the local bread store. Both women were weak from hunger and could not open the front door. They pushed and pushed, but the door would not budge. Peter's mother was not in the apartment to help them. She had not come home during the night. Wounded soldiers had been brought to the hospital, and whenever a new group of patients arrived she would remain at the hospital both day and night. In the evening Peter's mother returned to the apartment and found lying in front of the door the frozen corpse of a man.

Peter's mother brought her son to the hospital where she worked when she realized that his aunts were too weak to care for him. For several days Peter slept in his new home. After he regained some of his strength he visited the wounded soldiers that had been brought to the hospital. He and the other children who also lived at the hospital would sing songs and recite poetry for the soldiers. Some of the children tried to dance but were unable to because they were too weak from hunger. The soldiers would listen, watch and weep. Seeing men cry like children was upsetting to Peter.

On one occasion a terrible event took place while Peter and the other children were singing. In one of the beds lay a sailor who was large and strong. His entire body, except one arm, was wrapped in bandages, and he was suffering from pain terribly. As he watched the singing children who were thin and suffering from malnutrition he suddenly grabbed the bandages and ripped them from his body. The blood poured from his open wound, and within minutes he was dead.

In the spring of 1942 Peter became too weak to move. He would lay motionless in bed and would sleep most of each day. His mother feared that he would die if he were not fed more food. Her son needed sustenance, and she was determined to get him food. She acquired a loaf of white bread, a piece of butter and some sugar. She spread the butter on the bread, covered the butter with sugar and fed that to Peter. He ate it slowly. He hardly had enough strength to chew the food.

Peter's mother tried to provide her son with vegetables during the summer of 1942. She, like so many citizens of Leningrad, grew vegetables on the little plots of land that were available in the city. She turned the narrow grassy area that lined the wall of the military hospital into a kitchen garden, planting turnips and carrots. These are hardy root plants and can withstand lots of abuse. Peter waited with anticipation to eat the harvest. But during the long wait, he would go outside and eat the green grass that had already sprung up in the garden.

It was in the winter of 1943 that Peter would see his father for the last time. Peter remembered that he and his mother traveled by tram and then walked a long distance to get to the place where Peter's father was waiting for them. The meeting was brief. Peter's father wanted to see his wife and son before he was sent into harms way. Several days later Peter's father was killed in action. Peter and his mother knew nothing about his death until 1945 when they received an official notification.

LIDIYA (LIDOCHKA) KARASYOVA
JUNE 1941–MARCH 1942

Lidochka remembers what life was like behind the blockade in Leningrad. She was only three years old when her father left the family to join his comrades at the Soviet military front outside of Leningrad. Sitting at the table in the middle of the family room, he wept. He knew that he would not see his wife and daughter again. Suddenly he stood up, took Lidochka in his arms, kissed her and then set her down on the floor where she had been playing. As he left the room Lidochka's mother followed him and Lidochka heard her father say that her mother should take good care of their daughter because she was his most important treasure. She was his sugar. Lidochka remembers that her father would often address her as sugar, and she was fond of the nickname because she liked the sweet taste of sugar. After her father left, Lidochka lived and slept in the family room with her mother, her aunt and her grandmother. Even though the other rooms in the apartment had been closed off, the living room was still very cold.

Lidochka suffered for a long time from an illness. The little nutrition that she acquired from the little amount of food that was allotted to her each day did not help her recover from the illness. It was her grandmother who purchased a remedy and saved her life. She exchanged four rations of bread for one pigeon and then made bullion broth from the meat of the small bird. Lidochka was given one cup of bullion after another. Meanwhile her mother, aunt and grandmother who had given up their bread rations watched Lidochka slowly and completely recover from the illness.

Lidochka's life was spared, but her father would not survive the war. Her mother was notified in an official letter about his death. It said that he was killed on December 21, 1941, during the battle at Nevskaya Dubrovka. The battle was called by those who participated in it the battle of the meat grinder because so many Soviet soldiers died.

It was Lidochka's grandmother who went out each day to get the family members' bread rations. She would leave early in the morning when it was still dark, and she would not return to the apartment until in the evening. She would stand in line at the bread store all day long. Some days she would leave the apartment in the evening and stand in a bread line throughout the night to receive the family allotments the following morning. She would usually take with her the family cat, Pushock. She placed Pushock under her coat against her chest to keep warm. One day the cat disappeared and never returned home. It is very likely that the cat was caught by a hungry Leningrader who butchered the animal and ate it.

After grandmother returned home with the family bread the small loaf was divided into four sections. The section that was given to Lidochka was usually larger in size than the others, yet Lidochka would complain that her section was so small. Her mother, aunt and grandmother would tell Lidochka to compare the weight of her section with the weight of the other sections by placing them in the palms of her outstretched hands. Lidochka discovered that her section was heavier than the others. But the pangs of hunger in her stomach forced her to beg with her sad eyes for more and the women, though they too suffered from hunger, would respond by giving her a small piece of their sections.

In March 1942 Lidochka and her mother were evacuated from Leningrad. Leaving the city was a dangerous endeavor but crossing Lake Ladoga was even more dangerous. As they crossed by truck the ice covered lake, the Germans that flew overhead dropped their bombs. One of the bombs fell near the truck in front of the truck in which Lidochka and her mother were riding. The explosion of the bomb made a hole in the ice and the truck filled with children slipped into the water and under the ice. Lidochka remembers that it all happened within an instant.

The shock waves of the bomb's explosion threw Lidochka against the opposite side within the bed of the truck. Lidochka's head was gashed open, and the blood that flowed from the wound covered her eyes. Lidochka's mother covered the wound with her hand and stopped it temporarily from bleeding. When they finally arrived on the eastern shore of the lake a doctor performed surgery on Lidochka's head. Some of her skin was cut away, and the remainder was sewn together. The surgery was identified with a special name "children's military surgery." It sounded awful.

From Lake Ladoga Lidochka and her mother were brought by train to Moscow. The railroad car in which they rode was designed to transport livestock. It was cold in the car in spite of the small wood burning iron stove that had been lit. There were cracks between the boards of the car walls. and the cold wind that entered the car through the cracks blew out the heat created by the small stove.

At least one person in the railroad car died on each day of the journey. When the train stopped at a railway station along the way, the body of the dead person was removed from the car and left at the station. Lidochka was awakened from her sleep one day when her bandage became wet with blood.

The blood was not from her wound but had dropped on her head from a wounded woman who was lying in the bed directly above Lidochka. After the train arrived in Moscow, Lidochka was admitted to a hospital where she received proper treatment for her head wound.

VERA GRYAZNOVA
WINTER OF 1941–1942

Vera was one many young people who wanted to contribute in some way to the defense of Leningrad during the blockade. She volunteered to go into the air raid shelters located in her neighborhood and arrange the cots for the young children to lie on during an air raid. She stood watch on the roofs of buildings. If a piece of glowing shrapnel should fall on the roof she would remove it with iron tongs and drop the hot piece of metal in a bucket of water or drop it from the roof to the sidewalk below. This was done to prevent the roof from catching on fire. She visited the wounded soldiers in the hospitals and would try to assist them in whatever way she could. She would write their letters and would stitch together small pouches of tobacco for them.

Starvation would rage through the city in the winter of 1941–1942 and within two months Vera became a war orphan. Her father died first. Then her two brothers died. Their bodies would lie for a long time in the fire wood storage area in the back of the apartment building where the family lived. Vera does not know what happed to their bodies. Then one day Vera found her mother lying dead in her bed. She crawled into the bed and laid next to her mother in an attempt to keep warm. Vera was alone. The acts of war had orphaned her. She was just eleven years old.

Vera's aunt came to the family apartment and found her in bed. Vera was so weak that she could not stand. The aunt wrapped Vera in a blanket, tied her to a small sled and pulled Vera to her apartment located in another part of the city. When they arrived, they discovered that they had forgotten to take with them Vera's bread ration card. It was a disaster. Vera's aunt had four children of her own, and it was impossible for six people to survive on five ration cards. Vera's aunt sacrificed her life so that the lives of the five children would be spared. Shortly before she died, the aunt found some caring people to provide for Vera after her death.

Life behind the blockade ruined Vera's health. In the years that followed the war, she would suffer from ill health. Vera, however, refused to allow her family name to die. She eventually regained her physical strength and gave birth to a son. Because her grandchildren needed financial assistance, Vera worked until she was seventy-three years old. She, like so many others who survived the blockade, is not mentioned in history textbooks.

GALINA (GALYA) PLISOVA
AUTUMN 1941–WINTER OF 1941– 1942

During the first air raids over Leningrad Galya lost the ability to speak and move. The bombs that were dropped near the apartment building where Galya and her mother lived so frightened her that she lost the ability to speak. When the air raids stopped and it became quiet, Galya fell asleep to be awakened by a terrible noise. Bombs dropped by German planes had shattered the glass windows of the apartment, and they lay in pieces on the floor in the room. It was then that Galya lost the ability to move. After the thunderous noise stopped, a neighbor woman entered the apartment, wrapped Galya in a blanket and placed her under a bed. When Galya's mother finally came home, she called out Galya's name, but Galya was unable to answer or move. Galya was suffering from shock.

Later Galya was brought to an underground shelter near the apartment building. It was already full of injured teenagers who were students at a vocation school that had been destroyed by a bomb that was dropped during an air raid. The school was located near the building where Galya and her mother lived. Many of the teenagers were boys who had come to Leningrad from villages around the city. The boys were attending the school to learn a vocation. When the blockade around the city went into effect, the boys were unable to go home. Seeing the wounds of the injured in the shelter caused Galya to conclude that the fascist Germans would kill children as well as adults.

Galya would soon realize that the air raids were not the greatest threat to human life. Starvation was a much greater threat. The food that had been set aside by each family before the blockade went into effect disappeared quickly. The one hundred twenty-five grams of bread per day that were rationed out by the city government to most civilians was too little nourishment. People became desperate and would eat that which they believed would give them some sustenance. They used coffee grounds and made them into scones to be eaten. They ate the skins of potatoes. They took the outer leather straps on suitcases and boiled them into a jelly and added that to their diet. They ate wood glue. They bartered their personal possessions for food that was sold on the black market in the city.

Life behind the blockade became even more difficult when the water mains of the city were destroyed by German shelling and bombs. One day

Galya turned on the faucet in the apartment, but there was no water. It meant that she and her mother would have to acquire water from Zhdanovka River, the nearest river to the apartment. They would walk to the river; Galya would pull her small sled, and her mother would carry a pail. When they arrived at the ice covered river they would go to the back of a long line of women who were waiting to get the water from a hole that had been made in the thick ice. The ice around the hole was wet and slippery due to the water that had spilled out of the pails and buckets that had been filled by others who had already returned home. Some of the older women standing in line would slip and fall on the wet ice. Rather than get up to fall again the women would crawl to the hole, and with a ladle or some other type of device would scoop the water out of the river and into their pails. Some of these women were unable to get up, and as night approached they froze to death on the ice.

It was the winter of 1941–1942 and when people died, as so many did, members of the families would try to bury the bodies. A corpse was usually wrapped in a bed sheet or blanket and tied as a bundle onto a child's sled and pulled to the nearest cemetery. If the family members did not have the strength to complete the task, the wrapped body would be removed from the sled and left along the side of a city street. During the early months of the winter, government workers would pick up the dead throughout the city and haul them by truck to a cemetery. Later in the winter, the corpses would be left lying along the streets for weeks before they were picked up to be buried.

It was Galya's responsibility to walk to the bread store and get the daily ration of bread. In order save time and energy, Galya would shorten the walk by going through Zelenin's Garden. One day as she approached the garden she heard a man's voice telling her not to enter the garden. Galya looked up and saw a policeman. Galya obeyed and walked the long way, but on her return home from the bread store she entered the small garden and saw lying on the ground the body of a dead woman. Galya could see that the woman was dressed in a sheepskin coat, but her leather boots were missing.

In the days thereafter the dead body would be stripped. On the second day as Galya passed through the small garden she saw that someone had taken the woman's sheepskin coat. After that the woman's cotton stockings were taken. Finally, Galya noticed that chunks of flesh had been removed from the corpse. Galya knew that this had not been done by dogs because the people had already eaten the dogs in the city. She assumed that this was the work of hungry people who were eating the flesh of humans to stay alive. Such people had gone mad from starvation.

ALEUTINA (ALLOCHKA) IVANOVA AND "SWAN LAKE" WINTER 1941–1942

For years Allochka dreamed of being a ballerina. As a child she was taken to Marijnsky Theater to see the ballet performance of "Swan Lake." She could not forget how the small swans flew on stage dressed in white outfits and wearing white ballerina shoes. The dance that they performed was hypnotic and caused Allochka to enter a dream world. She promised herself that she would become a ballerina and dance like the small swans on stage.

After Allochka returned home she stood on her tip toes in front of a large mirror and saw a beautiful swan. She lifted the edges of her skirt and tried to repeat the dance of the small swans. Allochka's mother, Tamara, saw her standing in front of the mirror and joked, "You don't look like a beautiful swan but like an ugly duckling." Allochka was hurt by what her mother said and started to cry, but she did not stop dreaming. Allochka was familiar with Hans Christian Andersen's fairy tale and knew that in the story the ugly duckling became a swan. Allochka's father believed in his daughter's dream and would try to help her make the dream become a reality.

Mother would also support the dream and she sewed a ballerina dress for Allochka. By this time, however, someone had already made the decision to cruelly and harshly interrupt Allochka's dream. On June 22, 1941, Hitler's Germany invaded the Soviet Union and within a short period of time the city of Leningrad would be cut off from the rest of the Soviet Union. In the months that followed Allochka, like so many other Leningraders, was forced to the precipice of survival where physical strength disappears and dreams often die. Allochka, however, did not stop thinking about "Swan Lake." The eight year old girl remembered the dance of the small swans. She did not lose hope. The ugly duckling from Hans Christian Andersen's fairy tale suffered from hunger too, but eventually it grew and became beautiful and finally flew.

Allochka's mother worked in one of the military hospitals in Leningrad and sometimes she would take her daughter to the hospital. Allochka would assist her mother by helping her remove old bandages and replace them with clean wrappings. She gave her mother the clean cotton swatches, then she handed her the cotton threaded roll, and then she gave her the instrument that was used to take the pieces of shrapnel out of a soldier's wound. At first it was hard for Allochka to look at the blood soaked bandages, and to see an open wound was even worse.

One day Allochka's mother came home and announced that a concert was being planned for the soldiers in the hospital, and Allochka would be permitted to participate in the concert. Allochka was very pleased and decided

that she would give the soldiers a beautiful dance, the dance of a small swan.
Her mother agreed that the dance was a good idea and sewed together for her
a ballerina's skirt.

The day of the concert became an important memory for Allochka. She and
her mother walked to the military hospital and climbed the stairs to the second floor where she was to put on the ballerina dress that her mother had
made for her. She did not have ballerina shoes so she wore white gym shoes.
There were other performers who were getting ready as well. They tried to
persuade Allochka not remove her clothes because it was so cold in the building. Allochka was astonished. She thought their advice was strange because
she believed it was impossible to dance the part of the small swan without a
white ballerina dress. After putting on her outfit, she wore her coat over her
shoulders and waited for her turn to perform. She felt cold and her body shiv-
ered because of it.

Finally, it was announced that a first grader would perform the dance of a
small swan. The host of the show who made the announcement said that he
could not imagine how such a dance could be performed because there was
no music to accompany the dancer. When Allochka entered the hospital room
she saw that the room was filled with wounded soldiers who were lying on
their beds. As she walked to the center of the room the soldiers saw a young
girl with legs that looked like match sticks. Her short ballerina dress and her
headdress had been made out of rolls of cotton used to make bandages. They
noticed that the ballerina was so weak that she had difficulty moving her legs,
yet she tried very hard to dance. Allochka hummed the music to herself as she
danced, but midway through the musical number she became dizzy and was
forced to stop. She was so disappointed, yet the soldiers appreciated her effort and expressed their appreciation by applauding. Allochka did not have
the strength to walk home that evening so her mother took the little ballerina
in her arms and carried her home. Allochka's mother would never again call
her daughter an ugly duckling. From that time on she called her the blockade
swan.

Later Allochka was evacuated from Leningrad and brought to Tomsk
where she joined a children's club for ballet. At first the director of the club,
a famous ballerina who had been evacuated from Moscow, would not accept
her. When Allochka pleaded with her, she was permitted to join. During the
first two months it was too difficult for Allochka to do the physical exercises,
but she eventually overcame the difficulties and became a skilled ballerina.

The first part that she danced was a snowflake in a ballet entitled "Winter."
She wore an authentic ballerina dress, a crown made of cotton balls and ballet shoes. The audience applauded loudly following her performance. The
money that was raised through entrance fees to the ballet performance was

used to finance the construction of a Soviet tank that would be sent to the military front. For her participation in the ballet, Allochka was awarded a certificate of honor. The certificate was signed by the Secretary of the City Communist Party Committee. A picture of the Tank T-34 parked next to a high tower was printed at the top of the certificate. Surmounting the tower was a banner with an inscription written in gold that read "For the Mother Land, for Stalin." Allochka treasured the certificate and to this day has kept it in a safe place.

IREN "IREENKA"
FEBRUARY 1942

Ireenka's mother, Catherine, was a pediatrician and she believed that if her daughter was not evacuated from Leningrad she would die. She wanted to send her eight-year old daughter to her relatives who lived in the Ural Mountain region, but she was unable to accompany her daughter. Catherine along with other medical doctors had been assigned by the government to a military hospital in Leningrad. Her daughter would have to experience the evacuation and the trip to the East alone.

Ireenka would begin her long journey when her mother brought her to the back yard of a factory. In the yard the factory workers and their families were waiting for the trucks that were to bring them out of the city and to Lake Ladoga. Catherine did not know these people, but many of them did know of her. Through her work as a pediatrician she had earned the reputation of being a good medical doctor who was concerned truly with the welfare of her patients. She asked the factory workers if they were going to be brought by train to the Ural region. They told her they were not. Nevertheless, they offered to take Ireenka with them across Lake Ladoga and then place her on the train that was to take people to the Ural region. They further promised to ask the conductor of the train to look after her daughter. Catherine trusted the workers and so did Ireenka.

During the trip Ireenka felt her mother's presence through those who watched over her. Before the group arrived at Lake Ladoga the factory workers told Ireenka that her mother was an important doctor in Leningrad and whenever they introduced the little girl to others, they mentioned her mother's name. The people would respond by giving Ireenka a welcome smile and some of their food. When they arrived on the eastern shore of Lake Ladoga, Ireenka began her trip to the Ural region. The trip by train would take several weeks. On the way Ireenka had to switch trains several times. Each time the switch was made Ireenka was handed from the arms of one person to the arms of another person, and each time Ireenka was introduced as the daughter of the famous doctor in Leningrad.

The last phase of the trip began with Ireenka's arrival at a railway station covered with snow. The train conductor brought Ireenka to the person who was in charge of the railway station and then immediately returned to his train. Ireenka was dressed in warm winter clothes and had a large shawl wrapped around her head and neck. It was difficult for her to move her arms. In one her mittens her mother had placed a small piece of paper with the address of her relatives written on it. Ireenka took the piece of paper out of her mitten and gave it to the railway station director. He assumed that the address was to be Ireenka's destination, and he brought Ireenka to a man who brought her in a horse-drawn sleigh to a railway crossing. There they waited for another man who brought Ireenka in his horse-drawn sleigh to the community where Ireenka's relatives lived. Ireenka had arrived.

Ireenka and Catherine would not be reunited until after the blockade around Leningrad came to an end. By this time Catherine had received word that her daughter had reached her destination safely. She was sure her relatives were taking good care of her daughter. Ireenka missed her mother very much, and when Catherine eventually arrived she felt much more secure.

Glossary of Names, Titles, Terms and Abbreviations

Great Patriotic War. The citizens of the Soviet Union called World War II, the Great Patriotic War.

Komsomol. Within the framework of the Soviet Union's educational system students joined youth organizations that were sanctioned by the Communist Party. One of these organizations was the Komsomol (Communist Youth League). About one-third of the young people between the ages of fifteen and twenty-eight became members. However, membership among students in institutions of higher learning was usually high because membership would help a person gain admission into these institutions.

Komsomol members were exposed to intense political indoctrination and were expected to participate in all aspects of Soviet society. Members would offer their services to the armed forces if the government called for recruits in an emergency situation. They were also expected to work in a factory or on a collective farm whenever there was a shortage of labor. Members who entered the military or who joined an industrial or agricultural force were responsible for the political education of their co-workers who were of the same age group. The members had been trained for this responsibility during Komsomol meetings, which were mainly discussions and lectures of Marxist-Leninist ideology.

Leningrad. The city was the second largest urban area in the Soviet Union. It was founded in 1703 by Tsar Peter the Great and was named St. Petersburg. In 1914, after Russia went to war against Germany, the city was renamed Petrograd because St. Petersburg was too German sounding. After the death of Vladimir Lenin in 1924, the Soviet Union changed the city's name to

Leningrad in honor of Lenin. The name means Lenin's city or the city of Lenin. Leningrad became St. Petersburg again when the Soviet Union collapsed in 1991.

Leningrad State University. The university is the oldest institution of higher learning in the Soviet Union. It was established in the city of St. Petersburg on January 28, 1724 by decree of Tsar Peter the Great. Since its formation it has been known as St. Petersburg University, Petrograd University and Leningrad State University. In 1991, after the fall of the Soviet Union, it was renamed St. Petersburg State University.

NKVD. Narodnyy Komissariat Vnutrennikh Del (People's Commissariat for Internal Affairs) was better known in the Soviet Union as the NKVD. Its origin was in the All-Russian Extraordinary Commission to Fight Counterrevolution, Sabotage, and Speculation, or Cheka, which was disbanded once the Russian Civil War (1918–1921) ended and the threat of domestic and foreign opposition to Vladimir Lenin and his Communists had receded. The functions of Cheka were transferred in1922 to the State Political Administration, or GPU, which was less powerful than its predecessor. In 1923 the Unified State Political Administration, or OGPU, was created and during its tenure, which ended in 1934, repression against the people lessened. The secret police again acquired vast punitive powers when it became, in 1934, the People's Commissariat for Internal Affairs, or NKVD. It was not subject to Communist Party control or restricted by law. The NKVD was the direct instrument of Joseph Stalin for use against people in the Communist Party and country who opposed him and his administration and their policies.

Order of the Red Star. The order was instituted on April 6, 1930. Decoration with the order was made "for exceptional service at the cause of the defense of the Union of Soviet Socialist Republics both in war and peace time." The specifics of the decoration with the Order of the Red Star were later on modified multiple times. In the years of the Great Patriotic War the Order of the Red Star became one of the most widely distributed awards.

Pushkin, Alexander. Alexander Pushkin is recognized as the most important Russian poet. He was born into a noble family on June 6, 1799, in Moscow and was educated at the Imperial Lyceum at Tsarkoye Selo where he demonstrated his literary gifts. In 1817 Pushkin was taken into the ministry of foreign affairs in St. Petersburg. There he mingled in the social life of the capital city and associated with an underground revolutionary group. In 1820 Pushkin's association with Russian dissidents came to the attention of the authorities. He was exiled to the Caucasus; however, he continued to hold official posts. Pushkin was dismissed from governmental service in 1824 and banished to his mother's estate near Pskov. In 1826 Tsar Nicholas I, recognizing Pushkin's enormous popularity as a writer, pardoned him. Pushkin died on February 10, 1837, from wounds that he suffered in a duel which he fought in St. Petersburg.

Pushkin's greatest successes with the general public were two poems, The Captive of the Caucasus and The Fountain of Bakhchisaray, and a drama, Boris Godunov. Literary critics have decided that his masterpieces are the poem, The Bronze horseman, and the drama, The Stone Guest, which concerns itself with the closing love intrigue and tragic ending of the Spanish Don Juan. Of Pushkin's stories the most famous are The Queen of Spades and The Tales of Belkin, a collection of five stories.

Red Army. The October Revolution in 1917 brought Vladimir Lenin and his followers to power in Russia. Following the revolution, Lenin decided to disband the Russian Army, and in January 1918 the newly created Soviet government ordered the formation of the Red Army of Workers and Peasants. Leon Trotsky, the People's Commissar for War, was assigned to create and was appointed to be the head of the Red Army in March 1918. The army had to be established quickly as it was needed to fight the White Army that had been formed within Russia to remove Lenin and his Communists from power. Trotsky recruited a large number of officers from the old Russian Army. When he was criticized for this, he argued that it would be impossible to win the Russian Civil War without the employment of experienced army officers. At the beginning of its existence, the Red Army was a volunteer army, but losses during the civil war forced the Soviet government to introduce conscription in May 1918. At the end of the Russian Civil War, in 1921, there were over five million men in the Red Army. The majority of the soldiers were released from military service, but 600,000 men were retained to form a regular army.

When Adolf Hitler came to power in Germany in 1933 the Soviet government led by Joseph Stalin decided to increase the size of the Red Army. By 1935 the army had grown to 1,300,000 men. To every unit of the army was assigned a political commissar who was given the authority to override the decisions made by unit commanders if the decisions were in opposition to the principles of the Communist Party. The army also included members of the NKVD whose role it was to ensure that the army remained loyal to Stalin and his administration. By 1941 the Red Army had grown to three million men (three hundred divisions). Most of the men served in un-mechanized rifle divisions. The infantry was supported by horse-drawn artillery and a cavalry. The army also had two tank corps. They included the KV-1 tank and the T34 tank. It was the Red Army that would combat the Germans and the Finns as they invaded the Soviet Union in June 1941.

Red Square. The square is a bricked expanse in the heart of Moscow located just outside of the Kremlin, along its eastern wall. Red Square's history dates back to the days of Tsarist Russia. In the late fifteenth century, it was called Torg, or market square, and people came to the square to purchase food, livestock and wares. By the late sixteenth century, it was named Trinity Square and served as the main entrance to the Kremlin. It was not until 1650 that it received the name Krasnaya Ploschad, krasnaya meaning both red and beautiful. During Soviet times the Soviet military would display its might in May Day parades as it passed the leadership of the Soviet Union who stood on top of Vladimir Lenin's tomb built in Red Square.

Red Star. The Red Star was adopted by Vladimir Lenin, father of the Soviet Union, and his Communists as a symbol of the Marxist-Leninist state. The five points of the star represented the five fingers of the working hand. They also represented the unity of the proletariat living on the five continents of the earth. The color red referred to the blood that had been shed by the proletariat in their struggle against capitalism. The Red Star was also identified as the star of justice. Therefore, it became a badge that was placed on the uniform cap of the Red Army. It meant that the Red Army had been formed to secure and ensure justice for all the proletariat. On the star was placed a sickle and hammer. The sickle represented the reaper, the peasant, and the hammer represented the smith, the industrial worker.

Soviet Union. The Union of Soviet Socialist Republics was commonly called the Soviet Union. It was formally established in December 1922 as a federal union consisting of territories, regions, nominally autonomous states and republics. Of the four republics, the Russian Soviet Federated Socialist Republic (Russia) was the largest and the most influential. The other three were the Transcaucasian Soviet Federated Socialist Republic, the Ukrainian Soviet Socialist Republic (Ukraine) and the Belorussian Soviet Socialist Republic (Belorussia). The number of union republics and exact boundaries in the Soviet Union shifted over time. The Turkmen and Uzbek republics (Turkmenistan and Uzbekistan) were carved out of the Central Asian part of the Russian Soviet Federated Socialist Republic in 1924. In this same region, the Tajik republic (Tajikistan) was demarcated from Uzbek territory in 1929, and the Kazakh and Kirgis republics (Kazakhstan and Kirgizia) were likewise formed from the Russian Soviet Federated Socialist Republic in 1936. In that same year the Transcausasian republic was dissolved, and its three constituent republics—Georgia, Armenia and Azerbaijan—each became union republics of the Soviet Union. The westward extension of the Soviet Union borders in 1939 and 1940 enlarged Ukraine and Belorussia and annexed five areas as distinct republics: the three Baltic states of Estonia, Latvia and Lithuania; Moldavia, most of which was taken from Romania; and the Karell-Finnish republic, which included territory taken from Finland.

Swan Lake. The ballet was one of the most popular ballets performed in the Soviet Union. The music was written by Piotr Illitch Tchaikovsky, and the ballet was first performed at the Bolshoi Theatre in Moscow, Russia in February 1877. Following the death of the composer, the ballet was revised by the composer's brother Modest and the conductor Riccardo Drigo. The revised version received its premiere at the Maryinsky Theatre in St. Petersburg in January 1895 with choreography by Marius Petipa and Lev Ivanov.

Swan Lake concerns a prince named Siegfried who falls in love with a princess named Odette. The princess is in human form at night, but under the spell of an evil magician named Von Rothbart she becomes a swan at night. The lake where she lives was formed by the tears of her parents after Von Rothbart kidnapped her. Odette has a retinue of swan maidens who attend her. One evening Prince Siegfried, while out hunting, sees Odette dancing in the moonlight by the lake and falls in love with her.

Von Rothbart takes his own daughter Odile and brings her into the royal court. With his magical powers he makes Odile seem identical to Odette. Siegfried dances with Odile and announces to the court that he wants to make her his wife. At that moment, Odette appears outside at the window. Siegfried, realizing that he has made a mistake, flees from the castle to follow Odette. She disappears in the lake, and he pursues her and dies. The death of the prince breaks the spell that Von Rothbart has on Odette, and the prince and princess are united for eternity.

In the ballet a single dancer dances the twin roles of Odette and Odile. It is one of the most difficult performances because it requires that the dancer act out two entirely contrasting characters.

T34. The T34 was a Soviet tank that was provided with sloped welded armor to deflect enemy shells. It was fitted with a powerful water-cooled diesel engine giving it speed and making an engine fire rare. Its main armament was a high velocity 76 mm gun. Its greatest value, however, was its simple design which made it easy to manufacture and easy to repair.

Victory Day. The day marks the surrender of Hitler's Germany to the Soviet

Union and other principal Allied nations in Berlin on May 8, 1945. It was celebrated in the Soviet Union on May 9, the date when the surrender took effect Moscow time. It concluded the Great Patriotic War, and the day was celebrated each year with a military parade on Red Square.

Young Pioneers. Within the framework of the educational system in the Soviet Union, students joined youth organizations that were sanctioned by the Communist Party. These organizations included the Young Pioneers for children between the ages of nine and fifteen. Each school had a staff member who was to administer the Young Pioneer activities. Each class was a Young Pioneer detachment that was comprised of three to five units, and the detachment was led by a Komsomol member. The leaders of the Young Pioneers worked closely with the classroom teachers to teach the children to be conscientious students and good citizens. Nearly all recreational activities for the Young Pioneers took place under the auspices of the organization. The programs that the organization sponsored ranged from sports and scouting activities to folk dancing and ballet lessons. Most communities had facilities for these activities, and there were Young Pioneer camps throughout the country. Young Pioneers were exposed to political indoctrination, but it was usually limited to instilling patriotism and Soviet values.

When a child became a member of the Young Pioneers she or he would receive a red necktie that was to be worn with pride.

Bibliography

Pavlov, Dmitri V. Leningrad 1941: The Blockade. Translated by John Clinton Adams. Chicago: The University of Chicago Press, 1965.

Salisbury, Harrison E. The 900 Days: The Siege of Leningrad. New York: Avon Books, 1969.

Werth, Alexander. Leningrad. London: Hamish Hamilton, 1944.

——— . Russia at War 1941–1945. New York: E. P. Dutton and Co., Inc., 1964.